THE REAL ESTATE
RETIREMENT PLAN

THE REAL ESTATE RETIREMENT PLAN

An Investment and Lifestyle Solution for Canadians

CALUM ROSS
with Simon Giannini

DUNDURN
TORONTO

Cover image credit: 123RF.com/alexghidan89
Printer: Webcom

Library and Archives Canada Cataloguing in Publication

Ross, Calum, author
    The real estate retirement plan : an investment and
lifestyle solution for Canadians / Calum Ross with Simon Giannini.

Includes bibliographical references and index.
Issued in print and electronic formats.
ISBN 978-1-4597-3841-6 (paperback).--ISBN 978-1-4597-3842-3
(pdf).--ISBN 978-1-4597-3843-0 (epub)

    1. Retirement income--Canada. 2. Finance, Personal--Canada.
3. Real estate investment--Canada. I. Giannini, Simon, author
II. Title.

HG179.R687 2017   332.024'014   C2016-906327-5
                                                 C2016-906328-3

1 2 3 4 5   21 20 19 18 17

We acknowledge the support of the **Canada Council for the Arts** and the **Ontario Arts Council** for our publishing program. We also acknowledge the financial support of the **Government of Ontario**, through the **Ontario Book Publishing Tax Credit** and the **Ontario Media Development Corporation**, and the **Government of Canada**.

Care has been taken to trace the ownership of copyright material used in this book. The author and the publisher welcome any information enabling them to rectify any references or credits in subsequent editions.
                       — *J. Kirk Howard, President*

The publisher is not responsible for websites or their content unless they are owned by the publisher.

Printed and bound in Canada.

VISIT US AT

 dundurn.com | @dundurnpress |  dundurnpress | dundurnpress

Dundurn
3 Church Street, Suite 500
Toronto, Ontario, Canada
M5E 1M2

This book is dedicated to my mom and dad, who taught me the value of a dollar, the importance of integrity, and the power of perseverance.

TABLE OF CONTENTS

INTRODUCTION Re-Conceptualizing Retirement   9

PART 1   **Threats to Your Retirement and Solutions to Overcome Them**

    CHAPTER 1 Retirement Risks and Problems   17

    CHAPTER 2 Retirement Opportunities   41

    CHAPTER 3 Mental Modelling Flaws   60

    CHAPTER 4 The Portfolio Approach to Real Estate   85

PART 2   **The Power of Borrowing to Invest**

    CHAPTER 5 How Businesses, Investment Firms, Banks, and Entrepreneurs Think About Capital, Investing, and Wealth Creation   103

    CHAPTER 6 Borrowing to Invest in Real Estate   125

CHAPTER 7 Selecting a Mortgage Professional   149

PART 3   **Real Estate — More Powerful than Any Other Asset Class** by Simon Giannini

CHAPTER 8 How to Profit from Real Estate   159
CHAPTER 9 Understanding Real Estate Expenses   178
CHAPTER 10 Selecting a Real Estate Agent   187

CONCLUSION   195

ACKNOWLEDGEMENTS   201
GLOSSARY   203
NOTES   207
RECOMMENDED READING   209
INDEX   211
ABOUT THE AUTHORS   217

INTRODUCTION
Re-Conceptualizing Retirement

> Retirement: It's nice to get out of the rat race, but you have to learn to get along with less cheese.
>
> — GENE PERRET

WHEN ARE YOU TRULY RETIRED?

A comfortable retirement is the goal and promised land of nearly every Canadian. Even for those of us who see ourselves working in our later years on passion projects, we know that once we are not working full-time, our income will likely go down. If we're not working full-time, we'll require income from other sources to survive.

But what exactly is a comfortable retirement? Before answering that, let's answer a more basic question: what is retirement?

Unfortunately, many of us have a misguided concept of this important life period. The tendency is to think of retirement as the day, somewhere out there in the future, when we will quit working. But in reality, retirement should be the day when, if we so choose, we could quit working and would have enough assets to live comfortably for the rest of our lives.

I would add that we should be able to make this life change without lowering our quality of life. Sadly, many people just assume a lower quality of life comes with the package. Many Canadians plan to "downsize" by selling their family home.

Why do we have this failed notion of retirement? It makes sense when you think about it. Retirement has — for many decades — been thought of as something our employer would provide for us. We would do our part, of course. We'd contribute to our pension funds and put money in our RRSPs. But someone else would do the bulk of the planning. The pension fund would make the investment and dole it out to us in monthly stipends near the end of life.

Fast-forward to today, and the retirement that was once promised to us is nearly extinct. Sure, some government employees and a small selection of others will still receive their pensions, but for large swaths of society, that old idea of someone else providing us with a retirement is dead.

Everything about retirement has changed, so why hasn't our notion of retirement changed with the times? It's not when we stop working that matters. True retirement is when we've created enough assets and ongoing income (from those assets) to be able to sustain ourselves for the rest of our lives.

The problem with the old conception of retirement is that it doesn't reframe the problem as a plan. Retirement should be thought through and solved like any other problem. We do this all the time with much smaller problems, but we often seem paralyzed when it comes to methodically solving bigger problems like retirement.

Could you live the rest of your life off of only your savings and investments? If so, then you're retired. If not, then you're stuck working.

The answer to this question is completely subjective. First of all, how much income do you need? Some will need only $50,000 per year and others will need $100,000. So, the first thing we need to do is ask what we need in terms of income for lifestyle. Once we know the answer, we can begin to build a portfolio that generates the passive income equal to our lifestyle needs.

Honestly dealing with this issue is a great starting point. But seeing the truth of our retirement picture for the first time can be intensely painful for many. The numbers may seem harsh. We ask: how will I ever be able to create so much income? The goal seems insurmountable because we look at our past ability to save and how much income we'll be earning over the rest of our working career and wonder where the money will come from.

The problem is that many people never catch up in their savings. They don't get enough money into the market soon enough to make a true difference to their retirement.

The question is valid: where *will* we find the money?

Many have stopped even expecting to retire without taking a quality-of-life hit. Their plan is to sell their house, downsize to a cheaper condo, and live off the funds. Worse yet, thousands of senior citizens contemplate a more difficult decision: McDonald's or Tim Hortons? Not for coffee either, but to make up the difference between retirement income and expenses. While there are many different retirement goals, we can all agree that working a minimum wage job to make ends meet isn't part of a desirable retirement. Sadly, though, it will be a reality for many thousands of people.

Without the certainty of a great pension (which many of us no longer have), we must look for different solutions.

As a result of my finance education and two decades of experience as a financial planner, mortgage professional, and real estate investor, I've come to believe that the answer for most people will come from *borrowing money to invest* in real estate — and doing it as soon as possible.

Now, before you slam this book shut and call me a heathen, please give this message a chance. In this book, I'll show conclusively why this strategy is so effective and, in fact, why it might be necessary for securing a stable retirement.

If you're feeling skeptical right now, I want you to know that's a good thing. I urge you to apply the same skepticism to the currently accepted system, because it's not working for most Canadians. Think about it: we *expect* to take a quality-of-life reduction in retirement. Does that sound like a system that works?

I invite your skepticism about borrowing to invest. It means that when you are convinced later in the book, your new belief will be strong and stable. But let's take a look at why skepticism is the most common reaction I get when I mention borrowing to invest.

Our society implicitly believes that "debt is evil." I'm unsure how we maintain this belief while maintaining record debt levels, but we do. We have a bad case of cognitive dissonance, because even while we consider borrowing to invest to be "too risky," we nevertheless borrow massive amounts of money to pay for vacations and luxurious home renovations and to buy toys, like boats.

Pure liabilities.

Did you get that? We think borrowing to invest is risky, but we borrow to buy things that will *most definitely* never earn a return and in fact will continue to cost us money for years to come.

We have easier access to credit than ever before, and many millions of Canadians have large chunks of what I call "dormant home equity" that for some reason people have started to think of as free money to play with. Instead of treating these borrowed funds as play money, we should be thinking of them as a great form of investment funds available to us. Nothing is riskier than buying a depreciating asset, and not just for the depreciation either. There is a tremendous opportunity cost when you choose to wait to invest instead of investing borrowed money today.

The purpose of this book is to both inform you and arm you with a plan. Based on my thousands of conversations and years of research, I firmly believe that most Canadians don't correctly understand both the scope of Canadian retirement problems and what exists today in terms of clear solutions to these problems.

The first part of the book will underscore the problems and solutions available. In our current day and age there are specific (changed) conditions forcing many Canadians down a path toward retirement struggle. I'll address these pressures in the first chapter, and yes, it will probably sound dire to many readers.

But there is good news. Just as pressure mounts, new opportunities arise. In the second chapter, I'll show you why I believe these opportunities outweigh the challenges. This will set the stage for the rest of the book, where you will learn how to capitalize on these opportunities.

But knowing the problem and solution often isn't enough. Our subconscious minds have a way of sabotaging our efforts if we don't have strong mental models. In the third chapter, I'll identify and discuss these faulty modes of personal finance thinking so you can eradicate erroneous thinking and improve your financial mindset. I'll end the first part of the book in Chapter 4 with a discussion about how real estate should fit into an overall financial plan.

In the second part of the book, I'll delve into the first key component of the real estate retirement plan: borrowing to invest. I'll discuss how the modern-day financial wizards of the world think about capital, compared to the way most individuals do. Understanding this discrepancy will help you plan for your own personal retirement by mimicking their successful behaviour.

Next, I'll discuss the specific advantages of borrowing to invest in real estate and why it may be the most powerful financial tool available to you — especially if you need cash flow to service debt (almost everyone does). I'll close out this section with a discussion and set of guidelines for selecting a financial planning trained mortgage professional to help you achieve your retirement goals.

The third and final part of the book is dedicated to real estate. Real estate agent *par excellence* Simon Giannini will present a detailed discussion of how to profit from real estate. In truth, the benefits of real estate are made many multiples more powerful by the use of leverage. Through examples, Simon will show the mechanism with which the power of borrowed money is unlocked.

Next, Simon will walk you through a discussion of the expenses of real estate. No investment works unless the numbers work. Understanding these expenses will help you prepare to become an active investor.

Finally, Simon will end the third part of the book with a discussion of how to select a real estate agent. In addition to a financial planner and mortgage professional, a great real estate agent might be the most important member of your team. So this chapter is key to executing your real estate retirement plan.

If your retirement savings are deficient, then the time to act is now. Many Canadians simply can't afford to wait. The first step to action is knowledge, and this book will provide you with both the knowledge and the action plan to get started.

A NOTE ON AUTHORSHIP

As I have mentioned, this book is the product of two authors: Simon Giannini and myself. Simon is a true professional and has influenced my thinking deeply on all things real estate. He wrote Part 3, Real Estate — More Powerful than Any Other Asset Class, and his voice has had an indirect influence on the rest of the book, which I wrote.

PART 1

Threats to Your Retirement and Solutions to Overcome Them

CHAPTER 1
Retirement Risks and Problems

Risk comes from not knowing what you're doing.
— Warren Buffett

A CANADIAN INSTITUTION UNDER SIEGE

Canadians over forty are bewildered, because the retirement landscape looks nothing like that of their parents. Some of us are lucky and received a financial education from our parents. But the sad reality is that most parents aren't equipped to provide a great financial education to their kids. They had the best of intentions for us, but for most of us (especially lower middle class kids like me), our parents simply weren't capable of teaching us the financial principles that would work *in our own time.*

Who can blame them? Nobody can accurately predict the future, and the advice that worked in the fifties, sixties, and seventies doesn't apply now.

Following our parents' (and society's) advice, hard-working Canadians focused first on retiring mortgage debt, and only after accomplishing that did they start to save. This flies in the face of the time-honoured wealth creation principle known as the time value of money. The debt-pay-down-before-investing model worked in the past, but it doesn't work today and it certainly won't work in the future.

For us — the generation after the great retirement era — following an investment advisor's advice about balanced portfolio, Registered

THE REAL ESTATE RETIREMENT PLAN

Retirement Savings Plans (RRSPs), and mutual funds just isn't enough. Even if we sock away every penny after life has taken the rest, we may not be able to sustain the quality of life we've become accustomed to. The traditional retirement model is at risk, given shrinking yields on global assets and a declining savings rate. Actually, it's all but a thing of the past. Chances are you won't be handed a great retirement, have a great pension, and be able to depend on the Canada Pension Plan (CPP) to fund your retirement.

But that doesn't mean you will have to take a job at Tim Hortons in order to make up your retirement shortfall — not if you take effective action right now. This phenomenon — seniors working minimum wage jobs to make ends meet — is on the rise, but you don't have to be another statistic if you follow the repeatable steps in this book.

It's not about getting rich quick; it's about using the combined power of leverage and real estate to create a profitable, consistent, and predictable retirement. We'll get into the opportunities of our market starting in the next chapter, but it's imperative that we first understand the current retirement risks.

So what is causing this Canadian retirement malaise? We'll discuss several factors in this chapter, and they all lead to a single conclusion: **nobody else will take care of your retirement for you.**

This reality stands in stark contrast to what was true for past generations, when the combination of the CPP, defined benefit plans, and traditional investing options like mutual funds were more than enough to fund a retirement without a drop in standard of living. Retirement was virtually guaranteed.

Today the CPP is drastically underfunded, and the government's actions in recent years demonstrate the seriousness of this problem. The launch of the Tax-Free Savings Account (TFSA) and the raising of the retirement age from sixty-five to sixty-seven are both government attempts to alleviate the problem of the underfunded CPP. With our population getting older, the entitlement payments coming out of the CPP will simply overwhelm the payments into the plan.

Corporate retirement plans have also changed. Where defined benefit plans once ruled, we now have defined contribution plans. This makes sense given the fact that corporate returns on investment (ROIs) are on a downward trend. Big companies aren't willing to take on the risk of paying out entitlements anymore. This has been happening for years, and there is little reason to believe the trend will reverse.

This leaves the traditional forms of retirement investment to make up the probable shortfall of the CPP and corporate benefit plans. But this former bastion of retirement asset and income growth is under attack in several ways, too.

First, market returns are down. Bonds are no longer a viable vehicle for growth or even a safety mechanism against inflation. Bond yields are so low that they cannot be considered a healthy investment strategy anymore — rather, they're a glorified savings account. Second, the stock market still provides returns, but if you look at the ten-year averages, there is no denying that overall returns are down compared to the fifty-year trend.

In former years, reaching a stable and prosperous retirement didn't require taking personal control of retirement planning. This is perhaps the greatest threat of all to Canadians. Because retirement has been guaranteed for so long, we have become complacent and failed to invest early.

There's good news: a determined individual (or family unit) emphasizing investing early, and with all available resources, can overcome each of the problems mentioned here. Most people can even overcome their retirement woes if they're starting a bit late — but they'll have to use the tools available in order to do so.

But nothing beats starting early. When it comes to investing, length of time in the game will cover up any number of sins — as long as you stay away from excessive transaction costs.

As you read this chapter and the rest of this book, please remember that nobody will take care of you in retirement. The job of planning and preparing for a successful retirement now lands squarely on your shoulders. This book is designed to give you the tools to take back control of your own personal finances so you can enjoy your golden years without suffering, struggling, or having to work a minimum wage job.

FAILING TO INVEST EARLY COULD MEAN FAILING TO RETIRE

I've been fortunate enough to give hundreds of talks about personal finance, mortgages, and real estate investing across Canada, from teaching MBA students at two of Canada's top MBA programs to speaking to large groups of "everyday people" at major convention centres. I've learned many lessons from these talks, and I believe any speaker will tell you the same thing: as much as we try to add value to our audience members' lives, we probably receive more from them.

Of all the lessons I've learned, I believe the core lesson is about the general psychology of money. It comes down to this: In spite of our best efforts, we fail to think mathematically about money. Instead of calculating income, expenses, taxes, and ROIs, we act emotionally and instinctually. We allow the momentum of past generations to decide our financial future.

I've often started talks with a simple question that demonstrates the time value of money. You can play along at home by asking yourself this:

Would you rather have $1 million today or a penny that doubles every day for a month?

Keep in mind that attending a live event is akin to entering into a social contract. You often know that the speaker will try to disorient you, challenge you, and alter your perspective. With this social contract in place, you'd think audience members would expect a challenge question and that the correct answer would be obvious. When a speaker asks such a question, the counterintuitive choice *must* be the correct one.

But even knowing that I'm asking a challenge question, the audience's response is typically heavily weighted to the answer that will give them far less money. When I ask them to raise their hands if they would take the $1 million, a large majority puts up their hands. When I ask who would take the penny that doubles every day for a month, the number of hands that go up is a small minority.

I need to stress again that the audience will do this in spite of the fact that it must be obvious I'm presenting a challenge question. It's a tangible example of how we struggle to think mathematically when it comes to money.

Now, $1 million sounds like so much money compared to a little old penny, but due to the power of compounding interest, that little old penny is worth $5,368,709.12 by day thirty. If you want to consider a thirty-one-day month, it would be worth $10,737,418.24. In both cases, that little old penny has been transformed into a magic seed, and, not unlike a seed, we don't see its possibilities until it has grown.

THOUGHT EXPERIMENT:
A PENNY THAT DOUBLES EVERY DAY FOR A MONTH

Day 1: $0.01	Day 11: $10.24	Day 21: $10,485.76
Day 2: $0.02	Day 12: $20.48	Day 22: $20,971.52
Day 3: $0.04	Day 13: $40.96	Day 23: $41,943.04
Day 4: $0.08	Day 14: $81.92	Day 24: $83,886.08
Day 5: $0.16	Day 15: $163.84	Day 25: $167,772.16
Day 6: $0.32	Day 16: $327.68	Day 26: $335,544.32
Day 7: $0.64	Day 17: $655.36	Day 27: $671,088.64
Day 8: $1.28	Day 18: $1,310.72	Day 28: $1,342,177.28
Day 9: $2.56	Day 19: $2,621.44	Day 29: $2,684,354.56
Day 10: $5.12	Day 20: $5,242.88	Day 30: $5,368,709.12
		Day 31: $10,737,418.24

The typical audience response is instructive, as this is exactly what happens in the daily financial life of most individuals. Due to a failure to think mathematically, or a misunderstanding of compound interest and the time value of money, we make impulsive decisions that are bad for our finances. If we can't visualize compound interest and the time value of money even when the example is extreme (doubling daily), what chance do we have with the pedestrian conditions of real-world finance, where a strong return might be only 7 percent over an entire year?

Once you add in market fluctuations that result in paper losses some years and poor decision-making that leads investors to pull out of the markets, you end up with the shaky and often difficult-to-understand reality that most investors face. Because we fail to understand the opportunity cost and time value of money, we continue to make short-term financial decisions. We are willing to give up $10 million for $1 million. Is there any wonder why we struggle to take control of our financial lives?

Our mental models around personal finance are largely broken. Failing to invest early is the greatest of these weaknesses. *Business Insider* recently told this age-old story graphically using imaginary investors — Bill and Susan.[1]

Susan invests $5,000 each year between the ages of twenty-five and thirty-five, for a total investment of $50,000. As I hope you never would, Susan stops investing at age thirty-five.

Meanwhile, Bill doesn't start investing at age twenty-five. But he smartens up at age thirty-five and starts investing $5,000 per year (as Susan did for only a decade). Bill decides to make up for his failure to invest early by investing longer than Susan. He invests $5,000 every year between the ages of thirty-five and sixty-five. Overall, he invests $150,000 of initial capital compared to Susan's $50,000.

But, in spite of investing a third of the initial capital, Susan's portfolio at sixty-five is significantly larger than Bill's. Due to the power of compounding and the principle of investing early, Susan has $602,070, while Bill has only $540,741.

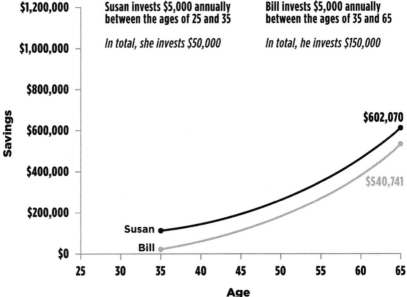

STARTING SAVING AT 25 VERSUS 35

Source: *Business Insider*/Andy Kiersz

But we Canadians are prudent folks, aren't we? Surely most of us live more like Susan than Bill? Actually, statistics suggest otherwise. The household savings rate in Canada has plummeted in the past few decades from around 20 percent in 1981 to slightly below 5 percent today.[2] There are a lot more Bills than Susans. Pun intended.

Bill is probably average. But on the lower side of the average, many people have next to nothing in their retirement accounts.

Failing to invest early is the biggest, nastiest risk of all the retirement risks. But who can blame Canadians for not saving early? Life is expensive, and many people simply don't have any cash left over at the end of the monthly bills. Plus, who wants to live a spartan life without some of the simpler enjoyments, like a family vacation or two every year and a car that doesn't squeal?

I won't (yet) talk about Canadians' tendency to borrow money to purchase expensive liabilities like boats and vacations. But even without these needless expenses, many people don't have the resources to get started investing young. Hence the savings rates are low. This is the changing nature of our personal finance environment. It sounds bad, and for many it is bad. But, more than anything, it simply represents a change in the marketplace — and Canadians need to adapt.

You can change your approach, however, so that you can take advantage of massive sources of capital that are just sitting there, right now, to be used. Tapping into this "dormant equity" will allow you to overcome this first major hurdle on your way to a successful retirement. It will allow you to invest early and, therefore, profit longer.

MARKET RETURNS AREN'T WHAT THEY USED TO BE

Here's an unpleasant fact: investment portfolio returns are down. This is a huge problem, since most Canadians have their (often meager) retirement savings sitting in an investment portfolio that is completely dependent upon the market.

I see this regularly in my business. New clients come to me complaining of the same problem over and over: "Where are the returns?"

Clients of mine (a couple I'll call Fred and Martha) came to me in a common situation. Fred and Martha have classic Canadian "good jobs."

Each earns an upper-five-figure salary — Fred as a sales manager and Martha as a nurse. Fred and Martha aren't huge spenders, but like most Canadians they have consistently used a chunk of their income for enjoyment. Their family has developed a taste for all-inclusive-hotel vacations in the Caribbean and Mexico's Pacific Coast. Along with their two kids, Fred and Martha take one winter trip to the sun every year and have even considered setting up a home there eventually. In the summer they remain in Canada (they live in the Newmarket, Ontario, area) but travel to Ontario's lake country for a few weeks every year. They live in a nice, two-thousand-square-foot home — by no means Buckingham Palace, but a home fit for a middle class Canadian king and queen. Fred and Martha also drive nice cars, not flashy cars, but they've always believed in the importance of driving a newer automobile for safety, security, and comfort.

I could go on. There is nothing unique about Fred and Martha's life. They are great people, and in addition to enjoying life, they have been saving for retirement. Like many Canadians they got off to a late start investing in their retirement portfolio, which currently sits at about $125,000.

Both Fred and Martha are fifty years old and don't have dramatic retirement dreams. Their goal is simply to retire at sixty-five without taking a huge hit in their quality of life. They can't imagine giving up their trips every year and would actually like to do more travel — like most retirees.

In addition to their $125,000 of savings, they are adding about $8,000 more every year. Expecting to earn 7 percent on their portfolio, they will have about $559,983.37 in the retirement fund when the big day comes and they stop working — in other words, they will have what will amount to slightly less than three years' worth of their current salary.

Of course, a few other factors will mitigate their retirement risk. They expect to pay off their home in the intervening fifteen years, and if the Canada Pension Plan is still funded by that time, they will begin drawing money from the government coffers.

Still, it doesn't take a mathematician to figure out that their retirement savings fund is light. Projecting a 10 percent return, it becomes a more solid $801,753.86, but double-digit returns are simply an unrealistic projection in today's market. Times have changed.

For Fred and Martha, the reality was beginning to sink in that they would likely have to sell their home and move into something much smaller in their retirement years. This is why they came to see me: they wanted to talk mortgage strategy for when the inevitable day comes. They were even considering selling their home early to pull cash out and add more to their investment fund.

Of course, I steered them in a much wiser and more beneficial direction. But the point remains that there are millions of Canadians like Fred and Martha who are looking at making a similar decision. The choices are grim for many. Taking a quality-of-living hit is expected for many retiring Canadians.

Fred and Martha were stuck in the same trap that so many of us find ourselves in — they depended on the traditional retirement system to provide them with everything they wanted in their retirement, but the traditional system simply isn't able to provide the retirement most of us want. Especially not with today's meager market returns.

When I first did my financial planning courses back in 1997, an aggressive projection of return would have been 12 percent. At the time we considered a 10 percent return to be average and, being highly conservative, we would have sought 6 to 8 percent returns. Today there would be very few financial planners with the gusto to put together a double-digit rate of return on any portfolio.

Simple math tells us that if the market returns are diminishing at the exact moment when many of Canada's coming retirees have meager savings, it reads like a recipe in a disaster cookbook.

What's the cause of diminished returns?

Let's start with bond yields. The low interest rate environment has meant that yields on bonds, which in the past have been a cornerstone of successful portfolios, have literally been cut into one-fifth, in many cases. Even as recently as 2006, financial planners and investors could use bonds as a stable source of 4.5 percent returns — not world-beating, but nevertheless a solid base to form the rest of the portfolio around.

Of course, going back further, bonds have traditionally provided much stronger returns, earning above 10 percent in the high interest rate environment of the 1980s, but other times holding around 6 percent consistently.

10-YEAR GOVERNMENT OF CANADA BONDS

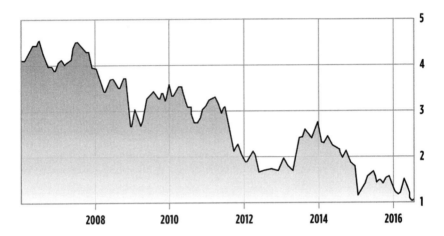

Source: www.tradingeconomics.com and Treasury Board of Canada

Today, bonds cannot be reliably expected to provide a return that even beats the eroding effects of inflation. The deteriorating condition of our bond markets has led to an absence of stable couponed instruments.

What is today's financial planner to do? Is there a comparable investment that will pay out a stable return to replace the job bonds once did? I'll argue that the combination of borrowing to invest and real estate is the formula Canadians must use to form the stable base of retirement returns.

Bond-market Armageddon isn't the only factor causing lower market returns for retirement-focused investors across the board. (Please forgive the hyperbole, but if a financial planner who had died in 1990 were to be magically brought back to life today, she would undoubtedly think she was living in a bond-market Armageddon.) At the same unfortunate moment in history that our bond market yields have all but disappeared, we're dealing with simultaneously deteriorating equity market returns.

If you were to look at the ten-year moving averages on our equity markets, you would see that the story being told is one of lower returns than in past years. Don't get me wrong; there have been worse periods, but compared to average markets throughout history, today's retirement-focused investors can't expect a robust 10 percent return on their portfolios as we once did not so long ago.

S&P 500 ANNUALIZED 10-YEAR PRICE RETURNS (MONTHLY)

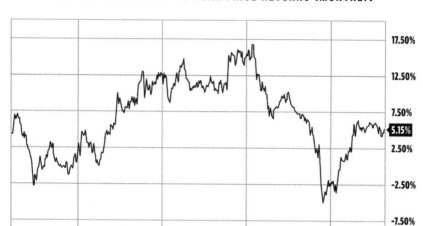

Source: S&P 500 and YCharts

When we add up the declining rates of return in the bond portfolio and declining rates of return in the equity portfolio, we are left with the fact that **the amount of money someone needs to sustainably fund retirement, both in terms of the aggregate capital base as well as what it pays out annually, has dramatically increased**.

Putting these factors together, we must draw the inevitable conclusion that investors need to put more money into their investments (hopefully at an earlier age), and at the same time investors must look at different investment targets. The solution is the combined strategies of a) borrowing to invest, and b) investing in real estate.

But let's continue examining the threats to today's prospective Canadian retiree.

THE CANADA PENSION PLAN IS UNDERFUNDED

Perhaps the most telling statistic about the Canada Pension Plan is that its founders thought a paltry 3.6 percent of employment earnings would be enough to fund the plan. Perhaps these founders didn't foresee the end of birth rates and the associated demographic cliff that our entire nation would fall off with the end of the baby boomer generation.[3]

We can judge by the actions of subsequent governments that it became clear somewhere along the way that the 3.6 percent contribution wouldn't be enough. To make up for the coming shortfall, the contribution amount has risen to 9.9 percent over the years.

By the mid-1990s it had become obvious that the original 3.6 percent contribution rate wouldn't be sufficient to keep up with Canada's aging population. The government commissioned a study that concluded that changing demographics, the increased life expectancy of Canadians, a changing economy, benefit improvements, and increased usage of disability benefits all meant that the (then) current system would be woefully underfunded. In fact, the study found that the reserve fund was expected to run out by 2015.

This led, in 1997, to a mandated increase up to 9.9 percent of earnings being contributed to the CPP. The employee contribution rate stands at 4.95 percent for salaried workers' gross incomes between $3,500 and $51,100, up to a maximum contribution of $2,356.20. Of course, the employer matches the employee's contribution. Self-employed workers must pay both halves of the contribution (9.9 percent). This is how things have stood since 2003.

When the study was undertaken in the mid-1990s, it was obvious that the entire fund would be dry by 2015 — a year ago, as of the writing of this book. This historical development is stunning in some ways, but perhaps not so stunning given the human penchant to fail to plan financially.

Our limited minds tend to think that things that have always been will always be. Of course, the CPP hasn't always been, but given our limited human perspective and our tendency to think only in terms of our present situation, it probably seems to many like it's always been there and that it would be there for the foreseeable future.

But some wise soul noticed along the way that this massive fund, upon which millions of hopes and dreams perched, was very close to drying up.

Thus the massive changes were made. Whew, the government planners really came through. Or did they? Putting aside the question of what kind of investment returns we could accomplish on our own with 9.9 percent more of our income (for the self-employed) or even 4.95 percent (for employees), let's consider the benchmark by which the government planners were measuring success.

Their goal is to have assets of 30 percent of the total amount of liabilities by the year 2075. I can't speak for you, but in my mind this doesn't sound like a stable amount of money, considering how much longer Canadians will be living in the coming years and the aforementioned demographic cliff of baby boomers.

In the rosiest of estimates, you and I will be drawing from the CPP in our senior years, but through more skeptical eyes (and this is the camp I sit in), the plan is nothing but a dream without more extreme action by the government. What will the contribution amount have to rise to — 15 percent? 20 percent? We can't put that kind of a burden on younger generations just to continue paying the old generation, the one that failed to plan for its own retirement. I consider my yearly CPP contributions to be a charitable donation to the Government of Canada (without the tax benefits, of course). There is no guarantee you will ever draw from the fund, and even if you do, it won't be enough to provide a solid retirement.

Thinking in this way might seem pessimistic, but it will give you a realistic base upon which you can build your retirement. By preparing in this way, it will become obvious that, rather than relying on the CPP, you should either pursue something more predictable and maintainable or put your faith in yourself and begin creating your own Real Estate Retirement Plan. Either way, one thing to keep top of mind is that the current model is not sustainable.

The CPP is in big trouble, and you would be wise to consider your contributions to it as a charitable donation without benefits if you are a middle- or upper-income tax bracket earner — if for no other reason than sound personal financial planning.

CANADA'S BIG BANKS: THE BILLION-DOLLAR QUARTERLY PROFIT PROBLEM

We've already spoken of the regrettable human tendency to not think long-term about our own personal finances. We look at our income and think, "Hey, I'm earning a good salary. What do I have to worry about?" We fail to see that in the future we won't continue to earn that same income and that our only saving grace in retirement will be the money we've saved and invested, not the monthly cheques we're currently earning.

But there is another human tendency we can and must rely upon when making our retirement calculation: greed. This tendency manifests itself in the mega-corporations just as much as it does in human individuals — after all, the mega-corporations are run by individuals, and, moreover, individuals whose main responsibility lies with their shareholders rather than their stakeholders. I'm speaking specifically of banks. Perhaps more than any other institution, banks are beholden to the almighty dollar — their own, not yours.

I don't blame them for it. Making money is their function, and so long as they're making a billion dollars per quarter, they will never change.

There could be an argument made for the idea that banks should be treated more like public utilities than for-profit corporations. Of course, I don't believe that. If I did, what kind of capitalist would I be? But thinking abstractly, it makes sense, since a bank serves a similar function to roads, public transportation, and hospitals. We need them for a well-functioning society.

When the roads are well maintained, we all win. If you own a flower shop, you need the roads to bring flowers to you in bulk, and then you need the roads again to deliver those value-added bouquets to all the lovers and mourners of your city. Yet the average florist rarely considers the roads a vital part of his or her business.

In much the same way, banks should foster our financial well-being. And in many ways, we treat the banks this way. Millions of Canadians don't think about the banks' role in our personal finance, and as a result we blindly plug our money into their system without considering whether there is a better way.

Let me tell you that there is. I'm not talking about Bitcoin, though. I'm suggesting that a little bit of rational thought and research goes a long way when it comes to our interactions with the banks. Remember that a Canadian Big Five bank is a massive institution. Each one earns a billion dollars of profit *each quarter*. (Only CIBC narrowly missed a billion per quarter in 2015.[4])

Hence the phrase, "The billion dollar quarterly profit problem."

Make no mistake: I'm not against banks earning profits, even big profits. What distresses me is the fact that they do so while providing only a fraction of the benefit possible to Canadians. And in many cases it could reasonably be said that the banks are a detriment to Canadians' financial health.

We must understand that no company gets this massive without a sales and marketing army. The banks' sales army is made up of those pedestrian-seeming personal bankers you visit in the back offices of your branch. They don't always seem to be selling you anything, but why should they? Their marketing force has already done it for you.

"You're richer than you think."

I don't blame the banks. You and I would continue with business as usual, too, if we were earning a billion dollars per quarter. There's no meaningful incentive to change anything. They are earning enormous amounts of money year after year in this traditional and conservative banking system of Canada.

If you haven't researched this topic yourself yet, you might be wondering, "How are they not serving us well?" Let's take a look at a couple of the ways.

Consumers Unknowingly Overcompensate Financial Institutions for Subpar Performance

If you were to visit a fee-based financial planner and they were to help you earn the same insignificant returns that you get from the traditional banking investment system, you would fire them immediately.

But instead of firing the banks, most Canadians go back year every year and hand over their retirement savings dutifully, as though they've been cowed by a schoolyard bully. It seems like a massive case of loving your abuser, but most Canadians just don't know they're being abused. Mom, Dad, Grandma, and Grandpa have always done it this way, so we continue to do it the exact same way.

Luckily, with the new CRM (Client Relationship Model) legislation in place, the banks will have to start revealing their fee structures more openly. This should help end some of the abuse immediately. But as consumers we should demand more — legislation or not.

We've plugged our money into the system and have received little in return, and often nothing. The financial institutions tell us to invest in mutual funds, but the banks own the funds, and they have figured out that Canadians don't ask a lot of questions when it comes to trailer fees and management fees, resulting in Canadians having some of the highest mutual fund management fees in the world. If most consumers recognized how much they were paying in fees on their mutual funds, they would pull their money out of this system and seek a new way.

We are left with this absurd situation: not only are we paying abnormally high trailer and management fees when we could get a comparable *professional money manager* for the same amount, but on top of it, we're paying those massive management fees for *subpar performance.*

Ignoring the performance of the portfolio for a moment, consider just the compounded returns that accrue when adding back the (as much as) 3 percent lost on fees alone. It's enormous. In a 2013 piece for the *Globe and Mail*, writer Paul Brent pointed out the absurdity of paying such fees. Citing Toronto-based advisor Kurt Rosentreter, Brent wrote:

> Mr. Rosentreter produces a quick example: a 40-year-old with $300,000 in his investment portfolio saving for 25 years and aiming for a 5-per-cent average annual return. That will grow to $1.015-million over that span (with no additional contributions for ease of calculation). Bumping that rate of return to 7 per cent, by dropping fees to 1 per cent from 3 per cent over that span, would increase the investment pile to approximately $1.628-million — or 50 per cent more.[5]

The insanity of the situation becomes obvious when looking at the cold hard numbers. But most of us don't have mathematical intuition. In fact, math is the opposite of intuition and requires deliberate, rational thinking.

For starters, many consumers don't even realize what fees they're paying and how much it amounts to. This situation should be somewhat improved by new legislation that requires the banks to disclose investment product fees, but for now most consumers don't seem very aware of the cost of these fees. Even for those who understand the fees, it's difficult to create a mental model for the true cost of a couple of little points over time. Over the length of an investment, one and two percentage points end up being very large numbers.

Most investors seem happy to continue to delegate their investment decisions to the banks' investment advisors — the same advisors who will undoubtedly continue to plug investor dollars into the same set of mutual funds that charge exorbitant fees, while ignoring lower-cost options like ETFs (exchange-traded funds).

They have to, because, as Paul Brent points out in the same article, "Some advisers are not putting clients in ETFs for a simple reason: They can't. Investment advisers licensed by the Mutual Fund Dealers Association are able to sell mutual funds but not ETFs. The smaller group of advisers licensed by the Investment Industry Regulatory Organization of Canada (IIROC) can sell individual stocks or ETFs to clients."

In fact, IIROC-licensed people can sell mutual funds, too, on top of stocks, ETFs, and many other financial products, while maintaining a much more rigorous licensing standard. In this way, the system of high fees is perpetuated and continues. Many Canadians seem okay to let the system continue in this way, but it can only change through the actions of individuals like you. I'm betting that you're tired of this situation, which is probably at least part of the reason you're reading this book right now.

Think of it this way: a fund manager would have to earn significantly better returns than the market to make his or her role a worthwhile investment to the individual, but the reality is that not only are fund managers not outperforming the market, *they're not even keeping pace with the market.*

Large percentages (86 percent in 2014) of fund managers don't beat the market.[6] Of those who do, how many do you think do so well that they would more than make up for the enormous fees being paid them? The answer is impossible to know for certain, but we can safely say that your odds of being better off by paying huge fees to a fund manager are very low. In most cases, if there is a way to eliminate the fees and simply keep pace with the market, you'll do far better.

But don't blame the banks. They're acting exactly as they should be expected to act. Each one of our Big Five is earning a billion dollars of profit each quarter, with no foreseeable change in the future. They will only begin to change when our actions as a group force them to. In the meantime, we must seek different solutions.

The crazy fee structure is only part of the problem. Let's take a look at some others.

The Product and Expertise Gap

When you go into your bank to speak to your "investment advisor," there is a very good chance that you will be speaking to an individual who, whatever his or her other redeeming characteristics, is not well educated as an investment advisor. In fact, the banks often only require their advisors to have the base model course, called Investment Funds in Canada. This course is offered by the Canadian Securities Institute, and the approximate hours of study required for it are estimated at 90 to 140 hours.[7]

Again, this weakness in the banks' service can be traced back to a single reason: a billion dollars of profit per quarter. Getting all of these branch-level investment advisors trained up would require an enormous undertaking that would cost the banks a lot of money. What compelling reason would you have to do this when you already have more assets under management than your non-bank competitors?

Furthermore, and dare I say a bit nefariously, the banks might find that the better trained their advisors are, the less likely they would be to push their own mutual funds. In other words, training investment advisors to a higher standard might (they seem to believe) cost them money in the long run, rather than make them more money. I would disagree, as there is always business to be had in excellent service, but the big banks don't always agree with me — especially when it comes to their investment products and advisors. It seems strange, though, when they offer so much additional value in their mortgage products.

A couple of decades ago, the banks seemed to realize that better mortgage products helped their bottom line rather than hurt it, so they began developing the sophisticated mortgage products they offer today. They haven't gotten there with their investment products yet, however, and they don't seem to see the potential return on investment they could reap by training their employees to a higher level.

As things stand now, bank-employed investment advisors are far more likely to be marginally licensed salespeople than true financial advisors. You might even say that the term "advisor" is just part of the marketing machine. By pretending to be big, stable institutions that have Canadians' interests as their top priority, the big banks are able to gain more trust. What seems more worthy of trust than a big Canadian bank, after all? It feels like they've been around forever, and they have big marble columns out front.

For these advisors to be truly valuable, they would need a more diverse bouquet of investment products than the mutual funds they currently sell. In addition, they would need the ability to proactively manage their clients' mortgage and debt-to-equity ratios in their overall financial portfolio and understand interest deductibility. But none of these criteria are being met, and as a result the people with the greatest need for solid investment advice are paying Holt Renfrew pricing while getting Walmart-quality investment advice.

At least half of the responsibility for this situation lies in banks' hands. After all, they must know how their system is affecting ordinary Canadians. But we can't place all of the blame on the banks. Canadians get to vote with their wallets, and we don't have to invest the money (inside or outside our RRSPs) with the banks. We could take our investment business elsewhere. This would force the banks to create better investment products and train better investment advisors.

So far we haven't done so in large enough numbers to force the banks' hands, but perhaps one day we will. It's frustrating from my position because I see the damage caused by the traditional investment system every day. But I also see how a little bit of personal education and some specific actions turn the victims of this system into the victors. Many of us didn't have a solid financial education in our youth, but today we are able to reverse that with some pointed lessons and focused action.

Intentionally (or Unintentionally) Confusing Consumers

Recently I found myself in a comical situation with two highly financially literate clients — a couple who were considering refinancing their fixed-rate mortgage.

The wife is a director of finance at a Fortune 500 company (with a finance degree and a Chartered Professional Accountant designation). The husband is a C-level executive at a large company (with a finance MBA), earning $500,000 per year in his position.

Needless to say, they are no financial slouches.

I was there, too. I have an MBA in finance and have spent the better part of my adult life working as a financial planner specializing in debt for wealth strategies within the mortgage industry. I've always stayed on the cutting edge, and there may be only a handful of people in the entire nation who know as much about mortgages as me.

You would think that with the combined brainpower in the room we could clearly understand the interest rate differential clause in their mortgage documents. The interest rate differential refers to the penalty you will pay when you break a fixed-rate mortgage. It shouldn't be overly complicated.

The couple wanted to break their mortgage in order to refinance at a better rate (and unlock some dormant equity to invest), which could be one of the best financial decisions they ever make. However, they needed to know the real cost of breaking their current mortgage so that we could do an accurate cost/benefit analysis. But, in spite of my specialized mortgage knowledge and their high level of generalized financial knowledge, we struggled mightily to make sense of the clause. I mean, we were flummoxed. It felt like one of those tests we've all written in high school or university in which the wording is designed to confuse.

You could certainly make the case that these mortgage documents were purposely designed to confuse, since banks don't really want you to break your mortgage. Keeping you in fixed-rate mortgages is how they make their money. So perhaps they *do* intentionally confuse people. I won't make any accusations against the banks because I don't know their true intentions.

But whatever their intentions, nobody can deny that interest rate differential clauses are incredibly confusing. People don't know the true future cost of breaking a mortgage. I remain convinced that if they did, they would be more cautious in making their mortgage decisions due to the fact the big bank fixed-rate mortgage products carry some of the highest "breakage" costs in the Canadian lending landscape. Even the government has recently realized there is a problem and has begun to reform the system.[8] It's still uncertain whether these changes will make an improvement.

The three of us eventually figured it out after much intellectual labour, but if three high-functioning financial minds struggle so mightily to understand legally binding mortgage documents, what chance does a Canadian with an average level of financial education have?

For the sake of Canadians' financial benefit, the banks should be more user friendly. But, with the technical exception of some legislation, they don't have to change because people continue to sign up for these mortgages and hand over their investment dollars.

Yes, we get upset with the banks when we discover what appear to be hidden fees and other ways they confuse us, but most of us don't know there are other options. Thus the banks continue in the same way.

CORPORATE BENEFIT PLANS ARE WEAKER

Thirty years ago, almost a third of workers had great pensions. Now only 16 percent do. You will likely have to do without. Can you afford to retire without one?[9]

In my role I get to meet people all across the spectrum of retirement preparedness. Luckily, most of the clients who come to my practice are quite sophisticated, but every now and again I meet a person who shocks me with their lack of knowledge about their own retirement situation. One such individual was a man I'll call Mike.

Not only did Mike have an overspending problem and fail to accrue much retirement savings, but he also showed a glaring misunderstanding of his potential for retirement pension earnings. Mike was a lifelong employee of a mid-sized corporation, working a logistical job. The unique thing about Mike was that his father had worked at the same corporation. Mike got his paycheque every month and didn't spend much time analyzing the deductions. Meanwhile he saw his parents living a wonderful retired life off his dad's pension.

Luckily, one day Mike decided to get clear on his retirement, and he learned that he had a fundamental misunderstanding about his own retirement that was based on his dad's golden years.

Things have changed a lot at his company between his dad's retirement and the present day. Corporate benefit plans have changed dramatically. Whereas once companies had "defined benefit" plans, they now have "defined contribution" plans.

Tales of years gone by speak of the golden era for employees retiring from a corporate job. In these yarns nothing holds a higher place than the defined benefit plan. However, in today's corporate environment, the defined benefit plan is like a unicorn. The youth, upon hearing such tales, think to themselves, "Is it real? Or just the fanciful dream of a delusional senior citizenry?"

Defined benefit plans are all but obsolete in the corporate sector.[10] They still exist for some public service employees, but they are nothing more than a chimera for corporate employees. These days they've been replaced by the defined contribution plan, in which the corporation takes none of the risk of ensuring the retirement fund is funded. In the defined benefit plan era, the corporation would guarantee a certain monthly payout in retirement. This, of course, was excellent for the retiree, as he or she could plan life expenses and reliably receive the amount promised every month.

This same security is not provided with today's typical defined contribution plan. The employee is required to manage his or her own investments and will receive payments only based on the returns garnered. Corporations now take none of the risk for paying out a long-term pension. Yes, they provide some level of matching funds, depending upon the plan, but it amounts to far less security than a defined benefit plan. The amount of pension received from a defined benefit plan is based on earnings and service in the plan. Importantly, the pension is guaranteed for the rest of life. There is no guarantee that a defined contribution plan will pay out for life.[11]

For millions of corporate employees, the idea of a guaranteed retirement is now a distant dream. But the mindset that someone else will take care of us during our retirement continues. This fallacy in thinking will cause a great many people to accept a lowered quality of life during retirement unless they do something about it in advance, like borrowing money to invest and starting today.

SELF-ASSESS YOUR RETIREMENT RISKS

Ask yourself the following questions to assess how many retirement risk factors you're exposed to:

- When did you begin investing in your retirement?
- Have you stayed invested, thereby capitalizing on the time value of money, or did you pull your money out at the low end of a market correction?
- Have you been continually adding to your investment account, or have you taken breaks?
- Do you know the total amount of capital you will retire with, based on reasonable estimates of portfolio growth?
- Are you depending largely on the CPP to fund your retirement?
- Have you calculated the real future value of your CPP withdrawals, taking into account inflation?
- Are you aware of the fees your bank is charging you on your investments?
- Are you losing a large percentage of your investment income to bank fees?
- Do you consider your bank's "investment advisor" your primary source of investment information?
- Are you knowledgeable about the entire bouquet of investment products available to you?
- What type of pension plan (if any) do you have?
- Are you knowledgeable about the future benefits of your pension plan?
- If you have a defined contribution plan, who is advising you on your investment strategy within the plan?
- Lastly, and perhaps most importantly, do you have a projected budget for how much your retirement lifestyle will cost you?

WHAT DOES THIS ALL MEAN?

My intention with this chapter wasn't to frighten you. Rather, I simply wanted to share the reality of the current retirement landscape with you. Retirement is a concept that has been taken for granted in Canada for a couple of generations, but today's reality of creating a secure retirement is far different than it was for previous generations.

To put it in computer programming language, most of us are running old software when it comes to our understanding of retirement. The situation has changed and there is one key difference that affects us dramatically: whereas, in times past, we could expect some combination of the government and our employer to ensure a secure retirement, we can no longer expect the same thing.

In fact, by reading the signs around us, we can reliably predict that large corporations and the Government of Canada are deeply concerned about an impending retirement crisis. The demographics of our nation are heavily weighted toward the elderly. We have a huge percentage of the population moving into a non-productive time of life, and the traditional vehicles for funding retirement *en masse* are in decay. The rise of the TFSA and the change in retirement age from sixty-five to sixty-seven signal these changes.

All of this adds up to one simple fact: **creating a stable and secure retirement without a lowered quality of life is now the responsibility of each individual.**

But you're reading this book because you're a self-sufficient action taker. Let me tell you without reservation that *there is some good news.* While there are contemporary risks to retirement, there are also some unique opportunities for today's prospective retiree. Let's explore these opportunities.

CHAPTER 2
Retirement Opportunities

Be fearful when others are greedy and greedy when others are fearful.

— WARREN BUFFETT

RETHINKING THE MORTGAGE

While there is no shortage of risks and problems for retirees in the new millennium, there is at the same time a set of opportunities unique to this time. But to capitalize on these opportunities, today's working-age Canadian must reorient his or her conception of the mortgage. In fact, using the traditional term "mortgage" almost forces us to retain our limited perspective on what these financial instruments can do.

There is the ongoing joke in mortgage circles about the etymology of the word mortgage: it comes from the combination of the two French words dead (*mort*) and pledge (*gage*). The joke insinuates that you're tied to your mortgage until death, like a marriage that gives you no joy.

It's only a joke, but this is how many, if not most, of us have traditionally treated our mortgages — as burdens to be destroyed at our earliest convenience. People hold mortgage-burning parties celebrating the fateful moment when they are able to finally retire the mortgage bugbear.

Through speaking to thousands of people on this topic and doing thousands more mortgage deals, I've come to believe that this mentality is inherited from previous generations, back when the mortgage was only a means to an end. The goal was to own a home to live in, and the mortgage could provide no more than that. Being at the whim of interest rate changes and the threat of the bank calling in the loan on short notice haunted our collective unconscious. But that was then. I firmly believe that, if you don't already, you will soon come to see things the way I do now: paying off a mortgage might be the single biggest financial mistake you ever make.

ASSESSING CONTEMPORARY CANADIAN RETIREMENT OPPORTUNITIES

A couple of recent developments make today's powerful mortgages possible.

The first is the re-advanceable mortgage products available to Canadian homeowners. I won't go into too much detail here because I don't want to spoil the revelation later in the chapter. But I will say that the re-advanceable mortgages available today are the most powerful financial instruments available to the average Canadian — by a wide margin. It's not even close. They are so powerful that their proper use can help you overcome all of the risk factors we discussed in the first chapter and even reverse them.

Sadly, these incredibly powerful financial tools are misused. Canadians, seeing their dormant wealth available, use the money to purchase expensive liabilities, all of which end up creating additional maintenance expenses and economic losses rather than significant wealth. With few exceptions, most Canadians should be using these funds to invest. Later in this book I'll show you the power and versatility of this leveraged investment funding strategy. But in this chapter I'll simply focus on the re-advanceable mortgage itself and some of the basic benefits of a leveraged investing strategy.

A second massive opportunity, which is connected to the first, is that we are living through a period of historically low interest rates. This means that — assuming the investment is sound — there has never been a better time to fund investments with borrowed money.

But I want to make a point very clear: even when interest rates *aren't* historically low, it is almost always a good idea to borrow to invest.

Historically low interest rates make the borrowing-to-invest opportunity even more compelling.

Later I'll discuss the context of these ultra-low interest rates and why our economy is poised to continue down the low-interest-rate path for the foreseeable future. There is a lingering societal belief that interest rates *have* to go up, but the reality is that they will stay low for a very long time to come, and I'll show you why based on the macroeconomic conditions of our nation and the world.

It's the combination of these two unprecedented opportunities that creates the power base for today's investor. The first step is to take advantage of the re-advanceable mortgage mentioned. The next step is to invest the funds, a portion of which should be in cash-flow-positive real estate in economically strong regions and neighbourhoods. This opportunity combination enables today's investor to build wealth in a way that was unheard of for previous generations, but it requires some financial acumen. The standard, uninformed consumer will never know about these unique and advanced strategies. For the reader of this book, however, it will become common knowledge and common practice to always maintain investment debt to accelerate wealth creation.

I'll also take a look at a third opportunity, the tax-deductibility of investment debt, a personal finance step that will convince you that borrowing to invest is a good idea. Once you understand the combination of these opportunities, I'm confident you will agree that the benefits, when acted upon, far outweigh the risks. This last opportunity — tax deductibility — dramatically minimizes the risk of borrowing to invest, so long as the investor takes all of the necessary steps for prudent investing.

We are led to the following conclusion: now is a wonderful time to borrow money to invest in real estate and to stay invested over the long-term. This strategy, when executed effectively, will reverse an individual's retirement woes and lead to a robust retirement. These opportunities outweigh the risks they present to retirement today.

THE RE-ADVANCEABLE MORTGAGE

When Lucy (not her real name) came to me fifteen years ago, she didn't have much in the way of financial assets or income. Her husband had just left her and for some reason sued her at the same time, claiming bizarrely that she hadn't earned enough money during the tenure of their marriage.

The lawsuit was frivolous, of course, and was eventually tossed out of court and into the dust heap of other frivolous lawsuits by a (thankfully) sensible judge. Her husband left her without any child support and a significant legal bill in addition to two very young children, but Lucy did have a stable job, earning in the range of $40,000 per year in an administrative position, and she was awarded the modest family home in the divorce settlement.

At that time it was a stretch to pay all of her bills and attempt to build financial wealth on top of that. She was up against the complex forces of economics and the battle of being a single mom in an expensive world. However, Lucy did have intangible assets that are difficult to put a value on. She was tough. She had a big heart, integrity, vision, intelligence, and focus. She had those qualities in spades. She still has them. I'm beyond proud to say that Lucy and I are still friends, and we still maintain a strong and healthy professional relationship.

What Lucy has accomplished in her post-divorce years — while raising two incredible and high-performing children — is nothing short of remarkable. Lucy has been a joy to work with because she quickly understood the financial concepts that other — often much more highly educated — clients seem to struggle with. She's not afraid to use healthy leverage to purchase high-performing assets that earn her a strong ROI. She understands the time value of money. She got into the market as soon as she could and continues to stay invested. Starting with only $20,000 in the bank, she's parlayed her small amount of money (but immense smarts and grit) into a total asset value of over $10 million and a net worth of more than $6 million. She's created wealth beyond what most high-earning individuals ever will.

But she's an outlier, and this book isn't even about making $10 million. It's about helping you create a stable, secure retirement without being forced to reduce your quality of life in retirement, or worse, being forced to take a lower-wage job to make up the shortfall between your monthly cash need and the amount you receive.

Lucy tries to give me the credit, but it's much more than I deserve. She educated herself, took the risks, took action, worked hard, and made all the difficult decisions. I just pointed her in the right direction and shared my knowledge where appropriate. So, sorry Lucy, if you're reading this. I can't accept the credit. It all belongs to you.

But I admit to teaching her an important principle that she was previously unaware of: **the principle of borrowing to invest**.

The principle was important but, moreover, at that time there was a relatively new financial product available that enabled Lucy to become an investor when, in years prior, she likely wouldn't have had the same opportunity: the home equity line of credit (HELOC). Essentially, a HELOC allows a homeowner with significant equity access to that dormant equity. The homeowner can do what they want with the money, and I strongly recommended to Lucy that she invest it.

Keep in mind that this was just after her divorce. It's years later now, and Lucy was an open book about her experiences when I recently interviewed her: "I was really desperate and depressed. My ex wasn't paying anything and I had the financial strain of paying my mortgage and taking care of two very young children. Everyone around me kept telling me I should sue him, but I wanted to stand on my own two feet."

She went on to tell me the story in more detail about how she went from that low place to become financially and personally empowered. Every day at lunch, Lucy would go for a walk in the neighbourhood near her work. During this low time she thought about how she could avoid becoming just another single-parent statistic.

She'd heard of real estate investing before, and one day on her walk she came across a home for sale. Knowing that some big parenting expenses were coming in her near future, she wanted to be able to afford the increased expenses she would face. She wanted to give her kids all the opportunities available to any child, and she knew this would mean tutoring and sports. That day when she saw a home for sale, a solution clicked in her mind. She thought, "Maybe I can purchase a home, collect rent, and fund my upcoming life expenses."

She did what most people do at this point, which is to contact a real estate agent and start searching for a property. In the meantime, she went to her bank looking for a mortgage and wasn't impressed with their expertise. It didn't take her long to realize that it would be difficult for to reach her goals working with this type of expertise. "That's when my real estate agent, Wayne, suggested I go see Calum," she said.

That was the beginning of a beautiful professional relationship and friendship between Lucy and me. She's one of my most cherished clients, which says a lot, because I love my clients.

Lucy didn't have enough cash available for a down payment, but she did have a home. She brought in her mortgage documents and property information to my office and we began analyzing her situation. The Toronto market back then was similar to today — steadily climbing. Upon looking at her documentation, it didn't take long before I was confident that, by using a HELOC, we could unlock about $30,000 of dormant equity. It turned out to be plenty of extra cash at the time, because back then you could still purchase rental property with as little as a 5 percent down payment.

If you're new to real estate investing in Canada, this will seem a bit crazy to you, as today the banks require a 20 percent down payment to purchase a rental property. But it wasn't that long ago when we could write 95 percent loan-to-value mortgages even on investment properties.

Lucy found a nice bungalow near Bayview and Empress in the North York district of Toronto. The property cost $250,000, which meant that her down payment was $12,500 — a not-insignificant amount of cash, but since we were able to unlock dormant equity for her, she was able to easily fund this, with extra cash left over. Lucy's goal was to maximize cash flow to fund the cost of bringing up well-rounded children. It was her biggest reason for getting into real estate, so her real estate plan had to reflect that.

In that way, her goal was very similar to that of many retirees. Both Lucy back then and today's retirees love market appreciation, but the true goal is a monthly income to fund life.

Before buying, Lucy knew she'd have cash available in her HELOC after the purchase, since her down payment was so low. So she formulated a plan to deploy the additional cash available through the HELOC to renovate the property and split it into two separate suites. This would drastically improve cash flow and free up the monthly cash she needed to pay for her life expenses.

Lucy tells this story with well-earned pride, and today she is happy to report that the extra cash and effort needed to support her children's interests has paid off wonderfully. Her son is working in the financial industry, earning a six-figure salary in his early twenties. Her daughter is currently completing a doctorate at the University of Toronto. Both kids excelled at sports, especially tennis, where they both competed at the university level. "There is no way any of this would have been possible without my investments," Lucy said. Math tutors for her daughter and private tennis lessons for both became accessible only after Lucy started to earn more money from her investments.

That first property was so important to Lucy, as it is to most real estate investors. The first one changes our perspective on how we can build true wealth. Lucy ended up holding that property for several years, only selling it recently. The little bungalow she once purchased for $250,000 sold for $1.7 million in early 2016. Since she bought it with dormant equity, her ROI on the property is incalculable, as she used none of her own money, earned cash flow for years, and sold for well over $1 million in profit.

But none of that would have been possible if she had been unwilling to borrow money to invest using conservative leverage. And, thanks to a basic mortgage product being used for good debt (the HELOC), she was able to complete the transaction. It would have taken Lucy several years to save up the cash because she didn't have any other sources for the money. The combination of her willingness to borrow to invest and the powerful financial instrument of her time, the HELOC, made her a wealthy woman. Better than relying on the government and her employer to provide a retirement, I'd wager.

There is a very real possibility that Lucy never would have been able to purchase that first rental property — the one that opened so many doors for her — without the HELOC. This is why I say that the current opportunities available to you can far outweigh the risks if you're willing to get a little bit of education and take consistent action.

BEYOND THE HELOC: TODAY'S SOPHISTICATED FINANCIAL INSTRUMENTS

Since the time Lucy purchased her first property, the humble HELOC has only gotten more sophisticated. Today we have re-advanceable mortgages, which initially started out as lines of credit behind mortgages. Through complicated accounting steps, certain financial planners started doing what's called a "debt conversion" strategy. As you pay off a principal residence mortgage, your line of credit grows and you immediately invest those funds.

Here I have to pay tribute to the great Fraser Smith, who made famous the "Smith Manoeuvre." Fraser was a friend of mine and was instrumental in helping get some of the proto-re-advanceable mortgages on the market. The Smith Manoeuvre refers to this debt conversion strategy described above. You maintain the same amount of debt, but rather than it being a debt against your principal residence, it becomes an investment debt. This accomplishes two things: you get more money into the investment market sooner and you create a tax deduction.

Fraser Smith's genius was twofold. First, he packaged this strategy as a marketable product, writing the first book on the topic and claiming it as his own. Second, he lobbied and negotiated to build the early HELOCs and other proto-re-advanceable mortgages we see today.

Keep in mind that the most financially literate and sophisticated people have always borrowed against home equity to invest. In years past it was far more difficult, confusing, and confounding. In essence, this type of transaction meant custom-building a combination of mortgage and line-of-credit instruments each time. There certainly wasn't anywhere near the flexibility of today's re-advanceable mortgages. Fraser Smith worked with Vancity Bank, a local Vancouver bank, to create the first re-advanceable mortgages so that his clients could do the Smith Manoeuvre simply and easily.

These financial instruments have progressed a long way from the early products, which we would call crude nowadays. The trend toward sophistication has continued until now. Some banks — National Bank, for instance — are offering mortgages with up to ninety-nine different individual segments. This means that, as a homeowner and investor, you could literally have a $1 million mortgage broken up into ninety-nine different parts. Although I'm of the belief that if you have ninety-nine segments, you have an unnecessarily complicated life. There's a joke in there somewhere about "ninety-nine segments, but a simplified life ain't one …"

I probably wouldn't suggest using all ninety-nine segments, but there is no denying the fact that these are incredibly powerful financial tools. Being able to segment the loan means investors can set aside different segments for different purposes. This is hugely important when it comes time for accounting, because only the portions of the loan being used for investment purposes are tax deductible.

Imagine securing an initial mortgage of $400,000 to purchase a $500,000 home (with a 20 percent down payment making up the rest of the price). For the first couple of years you are unable to pay off much of the mortgage, but in year three you come across a windfall of cash and, combined with your regular mortgage payments, you have now paid down the mortgage balance to $300,000.

With a traditional mortgage you would only have a $300,000 debt. You would be making progress in paying down the debt, with no additional benefit to you. The equity in your home sits dormant, with you stuck wondering when you'll be able to begin investing.

But with a re-advanceable mortgage, you now have $100,000 available to invest. Imagine you find a good cash-flowing property available for $250,000. You decide to purchase this property using $50,000 of your available funds from the re-advanceable mortgage. Since you have a great financial planner, you know about the importance of a balanced portfolio, so you take the other $50,000 available to you, seek your financial planner's advice, and spread it out across different investment classes.

With the re-advanceable mortgage, this set of actions would be simple. The mortgage is prepared in advance for this exact eventuality (and a million other variations). You have an automatic line of credit ready for you to carve up into as many segments as you need. Because this mortgage is so sophisticated, there is really no hassle for you, your banker, or your accountant.

Many people think it's risky to invest borrowed funds, but I would contend that it's far riskier to not borrow this money for investment purposes. Failing to borrow this money and then invest it wisely might be the biggest financial mistake you ever make, with the possible exception of the related problem — paying down your mortgage completely.

The re-advancable mortgage makes it incredibly easy to do all of this. What an unprecedented opportunity.

GET MORE MONEY IN THE MARKET SOONER

Throughout this book, you'll see various references to and quotes from the great Warren Buffett. Known as the "Oracle of Omaha," he is a true wealth-creation genius, and although he has created billions of dollars for himself and his investors via his firm Berkshire Hathaway, Buffett started his journey to enormous wealth through hard work and taking care of his own personal finance first.

By his twentieth birthday, Buffett had saved $9,800, which in 2016 terms would be more than $90,000.[12] Not bad for a twenty-year-old. Of course, Warren Buffett was the ultimate financial prodigy. The usual disclaimer applies here: results not typical. But the principle remains. Capitalizing on the time value of money is essential to building wealth. You and I may not be trying to become the next Buffett, but we are aiming for a safe, stable retirement without taking a loss in quality of life. To do so, we will need to take advantage of the time value of money principle.

The best way to overcome the pressures against Canadians to achieve such a retirement is to start investing early and often, but the financial reality for many simply doesn't allow for putting large sums of cash aside for investments at a young age.

Most Canadians purchase a home, which sucks up much of their available wealth. We attempt to fill our RRSPs, but most people don't have the disposable income to catch up on their RRSP contribution. For the average person, $100,000 of available room for RRSP contributions could be a significant source of investment wealth, but due to the opportunity cost of not getting the money in early, most of that benefit has dried up by the time they catch up — if indeed they ever do.

This is the ultimate benefit of using the re-advanceable mortgage, and of the very principle of borrowing to invest: namely that it enables folks to get more money into the market. It's especially important for those who were unable to invest young. Rather than slowly building up $100,000 or $200,000 like Warren Buffett, you have the opportunity to drop in midway through the game and invest the same amount (and often more). If you're five, ten, fifteen, or more years into the mortgage years of your life, there is a very good possibility that you will have an accumulation of dormant equity, which I call the laziest money known to man.

If this describes you (or even if you just want to accelerate your investments), borrowing to invest and investing a large sum of money might be the best financial decision you ever make.

Of course, as great financial planners would always advise, it's wise to have a balanced portfolio of investments. But in this book we're focusing more on the real estate investment opportunity and using dormant equity to take advantage of it. Keep in mind that if you purchase cash-flowing real estate, you will be able to turn your initial leveraged investment (20 percent down payment) into a property with five times more value, as the new mortgage makes up the remaining 80 percent of the value. This means that you're growing your wealth completely with the bank's money. There is no better strategy available to the aspiring Canadian retiree today, and it's all made possible by the re-advanceable mortgage, as well as the principle of borrowing to invest.

OVERCOMING WEAK MARKET RETURNS

In the last chapter, we discussed how market returns on a ten-year moving average are lower in this era than in past years. This problem is compounded by anemic bond yields, which means overall portfolio returns in general are down. It amounts to a disconcerting situation for prospective retirees. But by using borrowed funds from a re-advanceable mortgage, today's sophisticated investor is able to overcome most or all of the market malaise. You end up working with a larger amount of capital from an earlier time, which allows you to capitalize on the time value of money.

When you put all of these factors together, you can begin to see that the re-advanceable mortgage is the ultimate tool for overcoming the risks discussed in the first chapter and building a great retirement in spite of the challenges. But it's only when you combine it with the next retirement opportunity that the true power of the re-advanceable mortgage comes to life.

HISTORICALLY LOW INTEREST RATES

I was speaking with a friend from Alberta the other day and he told me an interesting story. Many Western Canadian kids grew up on farms, or at least one of their parents often did. I always find when visiting Edmonton that the entire city is made up of people from smaller Alberta towns who moved off the farm.

My friend was raised in a farming community where not only his father, but also many of his extended family, worked the land. He and I weren't talking about farming, though. We were talking about borrowing money and interest rates, of course. He told me the story of his uncle, a successful farmer in the area who had actually lost a quarter section of land (160 acres) to the bank back in the early 1980s. This wasn't a man who struggled financially. He had owned and operated a multi-million-dollar farm for decades already before losing this piece of land. His own father farmed and he had a solid support system. Everything else in his career worked except this loan.

My friend's uncle either owned free and clear title on the other pieces of land or had older fixed-rate loans on them, but at some point in the early 1980s he expanded his farm by purchasing the quarter section in question. Those of you old enough may remember the shockingly high interest rates of the early 1980s. It sounds dystopian almost, but it really happened, and it lasted for years. Just more proof that the economy and fiscal policy can create outlier events. My friend's uncle simply couldn't maintain the twenty-plus percent interest payments on the quarter section of land and he lost it.

Newbies in the lending, borrowing, and real estate space might have a hard time believing the insanity of those days' interest rates, but any student of finance knows just how real it was. Moreover, anyone older than fifty likely has a firsthand memory of the prohibitive interest rates of the early 1980s. I suspect that this history is a major reason for most people's intuition that interest rates "have to go up." It's true that they likely can't go much lower, but there is no good reason to believe that they will dramatically rise in the near term. There will have to be major changes before we see a big rate bump — even to historically normal levels. In the meantime, those well positioned will continue to reap the benefits of historically low interest rates for quite some time.

Whatever the negatives might be of historically low interest rates, they certainly aren't negatives for you and me, the consumers who have the unprecedented opportunity to borrow the cheapest money that history has ever seen — money we can then invest and turn into far more money.

HOW DO WE KNOW LOW INTEREST RATES ARE HERE TO STAY?

Low interest rates are not a short-term aberration, but part of a long-term trend.

— Ben Bernanke

INTEREST RATES AND INFLATION

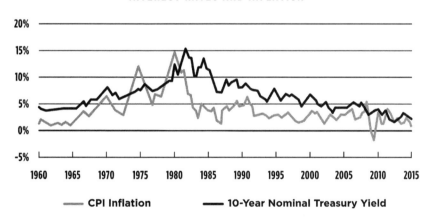

Source: Federal Reserve Board, BLS/Brookings Institution

To understand why low interest rates are here to stay for the foreseeable future, we need to go back to the basics and understand what interest really is. Keep in mind that when money is lent and borrowed, the lender is taking on risk and the borrower is seeking opportunity. The lender takes on two risks rolled into one. First, there is the risk that the borrower won't pay back the loan. Second, there is the risk that the money lent will be inflated before it is paid back and therefore be worth less than it was when first lent.

To compensate for both of these risks, the lender charges an interest rate. On the borrower's side, the interest is the cost of being able to buy something immediately without having the money. Think about Lucy. She could only buy property because she had access to borrowed funds. Borrowers purchase an asset that will have so much value as to overcome the cost of interest.

Because of these relationships between risk and opportunity, interest rates will always be a real reflection of complex forces such as supply and demand, inflation, and government policy.

Ben Bernanke explains the situation remarkably well (for being the über-egghead he is) in his blog for the Brookings Institute. People often think that the U.S. Federal Reserve sets interest rates, he explains, and that's nominally true, but the deeper truth is that the "Fed" is more reactive. They do set the interest rates, but their choice isn't arbitrary. Rather, they set interest rates based on what's known as the "real interest rate," a number determined by the complex forces mentioned above.

In other words, the real interest rate isn't a creation of the Federal Reserve or any other responsible central bank around the world. Rather, the interest rate set by central banks is only a reflection of the real situation on the ground.

In Bernanke's own words:

> If you asked the person in the street, "Why are interest rates so low?" he or she would likely answer that the Fed is keeping them low. That's true only in a very narrow sense.… But what matters most for the economy is the real, or inflation-adjusted, interest rate (the market, or nominal, interest rate minus the inflation rate). The real interest rate is most relevant for capital investment decisions, for example. The Fed's ability to affect real rates of return, especially longer-term real rates, is transitory and limited. Except in the short run, real interest rates are determined by a wide range of economic factors, including prospects for economic growth—not by the Fed.[13]

But let's talk in a bit more depth about just a couple of the complex forces at play and how they point to the fact that interest rates will stay low for quite some time.

Inflation

If you and I had a bond receiving 5 percent and inflation was flat, we wouldn't care to be compensated any extra beyond the 5 percent. But when inflation is high, we need to be compensated more for the risk we're taking. This is one of the biggest reasons that bond rates fluctuate: to compensate for the lenders' risk.

But inflation is remarkably low today. In Canada, it bottomed out below 0.5 percent in 2013 and today (mid-2016) is hovering around 1.5 percent.

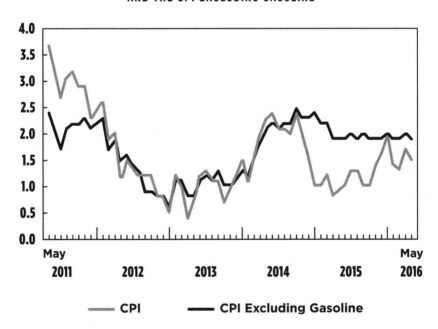

THE 12-MONTH CHANGE IN THE CONSUMER PRICE INDEX (CPI)
AND THE CPI EXCLUDING GASOLINE

Source: CANSIM Table 326-0020

Debt Levels

Our country loves debt, or at least it would seem that way to the detached observer. Why else would we carry so much debt in comparison to our rates of saving? On one hand, the situation looks incredibly grim.

We are a nation of debtors, since in recent years there has been growth in the availability of cheap debt. As previously mentioned, debt was once a necessary evil — a way to purchase a home when we didn't have the cash available. It may seem strange of me to speak ill of debt as I write an entire book around the concept of using debt to purchase investments and build wealth. To be clear, I'm not against debt — only bad debt. There are two kinds of debt: good and bad. Bad debt is any debt not used to produce more wealth.

In recent years, we've seen a massive increase in bad debt. People now borrow money from their lines of credit — which could, and I'll argue must, be an enormous tool for wealth creation — to purchase expensive liabilities. People are financing their luxuries. I believe in the long-term strength of our real estate market, but under no circumstance do I believe we should take a positive source of capital like a property and turn it into a wealth-sucking liability. Using a home line of credit for luxuries is bad, but worse is the common practice today of carrying a credit card balance from month to month, a balance racked up on luxury purchases and liabilities.

For many people, the low interest rate on their mortgage and line of credit is their personal Wizard of Oz. It works behind the curtain, creating and maintaining a certain image of wealth. But behind the curtain isn't real wealth; it's simply the illusion of wealth on the back of bad debt.

Many people do eventually end up paying off their credit cards — with cheap debt backed by their home. Better, but still not optimal. We are a society in love with bad debt, but our consumer debt problem is a tiny drop in the bucket compared to our government debt. If you think the consumer market is dependent on lower interest rates, go ahead and look at the balance sheets of the government of Ontario.

Here in my hometown of Toronto (the "Big Smoke") and the rest of Ontario, people seem blissfully unaware that we are living in the Greece of North America. Moody's, the credit rating agency, didn't fail to notice, however. They downgraded Ontario's credit rating back in 2014, and it has remained at the same level since.

The same story of ever-growing debt can be told across the nation. Justin Trudeau's new (nearly) $30 billion deficit is one of the largest since his father's era. But it's not just a Trudeau problem. Our government has run far more deficits than surpluses since the Lester B. Pearson era.

CANADA'S DEFICITS AND SURPLUSES, 1968–2014

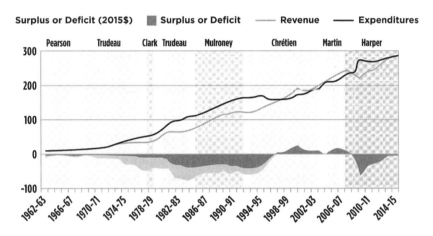

Source: CBC

Governments and consumers alike are addicted to debt. We can't seem to rein in our spending to the cash we already have. Of course, so long as we're using good debt, this isn't such a problem. But that's not usually the case, and when it comes to government, it's extremely difficult to measure whether the use of debt is creating greater wealth. Some government spending programs, like infrastructure spending, will likely pay off over the long term, but it's difficult to make an assessment on others.

The best answer to the question, "Why will interest rates remain low?" is simply that they *can't* go up. No sector of our debt-ridden society could manage to survive without cheap debt. There is a broad-based consumer and government dependence on cheap interest rates, and it will stay that way for the foreseeable future. Just as my Albertan friend's uncle lost a quarter section of land to the banks back in the early 1980s, we would see a rash of loan defaults unlike any in history if there were a sudden and significant rise in interest rates any time in the near future. The exposure to debt is simply so massive that a rise in interest rates would crush households and governments alike.

The Catch-22 of this situation is that low interest rates continue to fuel this debt cycle, since it makes sense to borrow money when it's this cheap. Again, I have no problem with that, so long as consumers are using this cheap debt to invest in assets rather than frittering this unprecedented opportunity away on liabilities (or, as the famous personal finance guru Robert Kiyosaki once called them, "doodads").

The major powers of the world recognize the situation we're in. There are few, if any, world economies that could survive a major interest rate shock. For this reason, interest rates will be kept low so long as debt levels remain historically high. Since this is the case, we would be unwise not to take advantage of the situation.

SELF-ASSESS YOUR RETIREMENT OPPORTUNITIES

Take a moment to reflect on the following questions, which will help you analyze whether you have access to the opportunities available for today's retiree:

- Are you currently using debt to invest beyond just owning your own home or vacation property?
- Do you have at least 20 percent equity in your home?
- Do you have a good credit rating and access to capital? When was the last time you pulled your own credit bureau report?
- Are you locked into a traditional mortgage?
- If so, do you know the penalty for paying it out?
- Could you take out a re-advanceable mortgage (also called a collateral charge mortgage) on your property?
- Are you younger than sixty years old and, therefore, young enough to ensure with reasonable accuracy that you have a long enough window to ride out any temporary market conditions?

To download more self-analysis tools, please visit www.realestateretirementplan.ca.

USING THE TOOLS AVAILABLE

In the first chapter, we discussed some of the risks faced by individuals today preparing for retirement. These threats are real, and the future holds some significant personal finance concerns for Canadians, but I firmly believe that in this potentially dangerous situation there lies an opportunity.

This chapter dealt with the significant opportunities that await the focused and knowledgeable individual. The evidence is uncontroversial: borrowing cheap money early in the financial life cycle and investing it wisely (and, therefore, taking advantage of the time value of money) is the surest path to a safe, secure retirement in today's personal finance environment.

But knowing this might not be enough to help you. Knowledge is power, but in so many of us there is a hidden psychology about money that sabotages our financial decisions. It comes down to our early conditioning around money and personal finance. The financial intuition we inherit from our parents and society doesn't equip us to make complex financial decisions.

The next chapter will be all about the mental modelling flaws that we unknowingly carry through life. In past eras these flaws of thinking weren't so damaging to our long-term well-being, since the large corporations we worked for, coupled with our government, took care of us in retirement. But this cradle-to-grave care is no longer a feasible method of retirement. Today we must plan and prepare (and, most importantly, take action) to secure our own retirement. To take action properly, we must address the internal sabotaging that I'll call "mental modelling flaws."

CHAPTER 3
Mental Modelling Flaws

What is elementary, worldly wisdom? Well, the first rule is that you can't really know anything if you just remember isolated facts and try to bang 'em back. If the facts don't hang together on a latticework of theory, you don't have them in a usable form.

— CHARLIE MUNGER

HOW WE FAIL IN PERSONAL FINANCE

Merely knowing about the risks and opportunities of contemporary retirement doesn't do much good to the individual if he or she doesn't have a winning mental model around personal finance. The phrase, "If you can't see it, you can't be it," resonates here. Due to familial and societal false beliefs around money, retirement, and wealth creation, most of us are stuck in a false paradigm not of our making.

Indeed, most of us never bother to examine our inherited money paradigm, so we end up with a series of subconscious beliefs that sabotage wealth creation efforts. We believe those old canards like "Pay off your mortgage before you start investing," even when this practice will effectively end our retirement dreams before they start.

We have a hard time visualizing wealth, so we find ourselves unable to produce it. Canadians are stuck in this broken paradigm in spite of the fact that there have been so many changes in our world, our nation, and our economy. Folks still seem to think we live in the late industrial era, where the government and corporations will hand us the retirement of our dreams.

Our false societal beliefs around money and wealth creation are many, but perhaps the greatest of them are the following:

- Having a fear of borrowing to invest.
- Making short-term, impulsive investment decisions and, therefore, always mistiming the market.
- Misunderstanding how and why real estate works and, therefore, refusing to invest in it, despite the fact that personal residences are the best assets we own.
- Having tunnel vision about paying down debt, which results in massive missed-opportunity cost.
- Making image-based financial decisions (otherwise known as "keeping up with the Joneses") and thus continually spending money on liabilities year after year.

I'm passionate about financial education for kids. I firmly believe that twin educations in money and health are the things most dramatically missing from our school system. We could alleviate the lion's share of heartbreak, pain, and suffering in our otherwise highly advanced society by putting far more emphasis on these life skills than on some of the other things we learn at school. The situation is often dire. Take me as an example. I was an eager student, showing an aptitude for mathematics and an eagerness for all things finance at an early age. Yet I graduated high school not knowing how to balance a chequebook, much less performing more complex personal finance operations like investment and tax planning.

However, I did learn how to make a birdhouse in shop class and how to sew my own stuffed animal in home studies class. Few absurdities demonstrate how woefully out of date our education system is than these sad facts. It would be more laughable if such errors weren't so widespread.

My cohort and I were trained for industrial jobs that don't even exist today. We were not even made aware of the complex set of tasks and mental modelling patterns required by a fully functioning member of today's society.

Thankfully, and in spite of our education, many of us go on to learn the rudiments of personal finance. But it could be so much better. We could be studying investment principles, tax planning, or the foundations of budgeting, at the very least. Schools fail to teach us the successful principles of personal finance, perhaps because there are so few adults who understand and use these timeless principles in their own lives.

In many ways the industrial model of government and corporate pensions has spoiled us for personal finance. We grew up learning that all we had to do was learn a skill or trade and work in that trade, and then the finances would be taken care of for us. But that's no longer true — if indeed it ever was. Today we need to take control of our own finances if we want to create a solid retirement.

But what about parents?

Where the schools fail us, shouldn't parents pick up the personal finance education slack? Perhaps they should, but again most face the same problem. Few are knowledgeable enough to teach the principles that they themselves were never taught. Most informal financial education passed from one generation to the next is either outright false or at very best incorrect for today's paradigm. Those old canards I mentioned are passed along from generation to generation without much thought. There may have been a time when debt was evil, back when lenders routinely called in loans at the most inopportune time and when interest rates commonly included first-born children and left hands. But today the lending environment is very different. Debt may be the greatest personal finance tool available to each of us when used to buy positive cash flow, appreciating assets.

The relative evilness of debt is only one of the many commonly received beliefs worth examining. How many of these false personal finance beliefs do you have? In this chapter I'll examine those I've seen most often. I'll go through these damaging false beliefs one by one and discuss how each of them is hurting its holder.

Fear of Borrowing to Invest

I love when multi-millionaires come into my office to discuss mortgages. What? Why would a multi-millionaire need a mortgage? This is a reasonable question to ask. As Canadians we love to be reasonable. This, of course, has benefits as well as drawbacks. Being reasonable in this case means more of the same — remaining stuck in that old paradigm of wealth and all that paradigm entails.

In this circumstance, we might be better off perking our ears up and paying attention to what the multi-millionaires in question are doing.

Recently, a very successful couple came into my office looking to purchase their dream home. The husband, Ben, is a CEO of his own mid-sized investment firm. In other words, he's a man who understands the principles of finance.

Short aside: Understanding the principles of finance doesn't guarantee that an individual will apply the same success principles in his or her own life. I've seen many finance MBAs who don't. They're world class at optimizing shareholder value, but they fail to create wealth in their own life — simply by not heeding the knowledge that got them to the top of the finance game.

Back to Ben: He and his wife, Anjali, were about to purchase their $4 million dream home. They had enough cash and available assets that they could purchase the home with cash only. But they didn't want to do that, instead opting to finance the property.

Why?

As we sat together in the conference room chatting about personal finance and their dreams, Ben said, "I looked at the mortgage interest rates and realized it makes perfect sense to take out a mortgage on this property. If I were selecting this investment for my firm, I would recommend purchasing it with debt rather than equity."

I sat there grinning because I knew a bit of his backstory. Ben's family did not have a lot of money when he was growing up. He'd worked his butt off, graduating at the top of his class at U of T and eventually getting an MBA from a prestigious American university that rhymes with Shmarvard. He came back home to Toronto, started his own investment firm, busted his butt, and succeeded wildly beyond his dreams. Perhaps if he'd come from money, he wouldn't have been thinking opportunistically about the purchase of his dream home.

Whatever the reasons, letting a golden opportunity like that pass by seemed ludicrous to him. In his high-level financial mind, he saw a chance to capitalize on an opportunity to invest a big chunk of money at a low interest rate.

Ben said, "I can secure a mortgage for two and a half percent, but after deducting the interest off my taxes, it amounts to only one and a quarter percent. It would be insane not to use that capital."

In his "day job," Ben consistently earns returns that dramatically outpace the meager 1.25 percent that it would cost to borrow money. So he and Anjali put together a combination of the cash they had on hand along with the proceeds of stock sales. They then took this money and purchased the house with cash. Immediately upon closing the sale, they came back to me, where I had the maximum allowable mortgage waiting for them. If you're doing the math at home, 80 percent of $4.0 million is $3.2 million.

They believed that not having debt at that price would be silly. Borrowing to invest isn't risky. The true risk would have been immensely higher if they had not borrowed to invest. Just paying cash and not carrying any debt would have created a huge lost opportunity cost, which is unacceptable to someone well versed in the principles of wealth creation.

Ben and Anjali then took that $3.2 million and re-invested it. To be honest, I didn't even ask them how they were planning on investing it. They didn't need my help on that end, and I was thrilled that they would be able to earn a spread on that much money.

Hearing these big numbers might make this seem like an abstract concept. But please don't write off their plan as a luxury of the rich. Anyone with significant equity in a home is able to do this in today's lending environment. It may not be $3.2 million, but there are millions of Canadians who could use this same strategy, a huge portion of whom have more than $100,000 of dormant equity.

It's a case of the rich getting richer while the middle class remains in the same cycle due to an unwillingness to borrow money for the purpose of investment. I find it particularly ironic that people are unwilling to borrow to invest, thinking it's "risky," at the same time they borrow to purchase pure liabilities.

Let's look five years into the future at Ben and Anjali's potential earnings on their borrowed money. Remember that they secured a mortgage at 2.5 percent, but since they can deduct the mortgage expense from their taxes, the real after-tax cost of borrowing is only 1.25 percent (a 50 percent deduction because they're in the top tax bracket).

Being conservative, we can assume they would earn 7 percent on their investment portfolio. Seven percent minus 1.25 percent equals a 5.75 percent return on investment. Compounding for five years, this means their $3.2 million investment would turn into $4,232,060.41.

Simply remarkable.

In five years, this couple will earn more money than some people do in a lifetime. Of course, things start to get a bit complicated when you start calculating after-tax rates of return (depending on the investment type and its corresponding tax implications) and other factors. That's why Ben and Anjali employ a great financial planner to help guide them through all the investment intricacies. They also have me on their team to actively manage their mortgage.

But let's take a look at a more typical example, the type of situation millions of Canadians find themselves in. Imagine a couple with $100,000 of dormant equity in their home. After five years, this second couple's investment nest egg would grow to $132,251.89 using the same assumptions that we did with the wealthy couple. After ten years it would be $174,905.62. After twenty it would swell to $305,919.75.

That's simply the return on investment of the initial $100,000. Of course, we're going to advise in this book that they invest in real estate, which would mean they're likely to earn far greater than 7 percent. And they're going to take several other successful actions that will help them create wealth along the way, not least of which is the fact that their home value will grow significantly over that time, unlocking more dormant equity that they can then add to their investment pile.

It's reasonable to assume that after ten years they would add another $100,000 on top of the $174,905.62. Then, by recalculating at the end of twenty years, they would have $480,825.37 rather than $305,919.75.

Sadly, most people will never take advantage of this windfall. We refuse to borrow to invest. Why?

The Momentum of History

Why are Canadians fearful of borrowing to invest? We live in a society in which borrowing for pure liabilities is considered normal and borrowing to invest in wealth-creating assets is considered risky.

You might reasonably say, "But you might lose all your money and then you'd really be in trouble." This "total loss" scenario seems to be the gravest concern of most people. But again, this is a case of people failing to question their assumptions. The reality is that wisely chosen investments, overseen by a top-notch financial planner, will almost never lose money given a long enough window of time. A loss on paper isn't the same as a real loss if we can hang in there.

If you're buying a real estate asset for a long-term hold and cash flow, it means that value only matters three times: when buying, when selling, and perhaps when refinancing.

Recently, my personal real estate holdings (and the whole market) in Edmonton took a hit due to the falling value of oil. I've spoken to several people who took great pains to point my "losses" out to me. But I don't care about paper losses. I'm only forty-three years old and (fingers crossed) still have a few good years left in me. The real estate I own in Edmonton is a long-term (forever) holding plan. I'm confident that I will regain all my lost value and then some between now and the time my kids have to make a decision on their inherited Edmonton portfolio.

The "total loss" scenario is an especially perplexing phenomenon for people who borrow for pure liabilities, in which you're guaranteed to take a massive (if not total) loss, to be concerned about. But even on more pedestrian matters of borrowing, such as taking out a mortgage to purchase a home, we are often paralyzed by our inability to foresee the benefits of borrowing to invest. Canadians purchase a home to live in, and, over the course of several years, the home that provides a safe and secure place to live also becomes the greatest wealth creation vehicle at their disposal. It's a home first and investment second, and somehow in the mix we remain committed to this idea that a mortgage is merely a necessary evil. For contemporary Canadians, the mortgage must be reimagined as the greatest tool in an arsenal of financial weapons.

The Canadian financial system comes from a conservative British tradition, and for a long time borrowing for any reason wasn't very common. Banks weren't even allowed in the residential mortgage market until the Bank Act of 1954. There's a deep conservatism around borrowing in this country, and the idea of borrowing to invest is absurd to many of us. There is a momentum of history at play here.

It reminds me of the QWERTY keyboard story. Take a look at the nearest keyboard. Starting from the top left letter on the keyboard, you will see the letters spell "QWERTY." Hence the nickname for the standard keyboard that was first arranged by the inventor of the typewriter, Christopher Sholes.

Why did he arrange the keys this way? Subsequent detailed studies show that the QWERTY arrangement is highly inefficient. All of the most commonly used keys are spread around the keyboard in a finger-contorting way. Many of these letters aren't on the middle line, where they could be most easily accessed without moving the hand too much.

It seems counterproductive, but there was a good reason for this arrangement. Back in the early days of the typewriter, jamming keys was a common problem. The only way to stop the jamming was to make sure the last letter had gone back to its place before the next one came sailing toward the paper. Slower typing was a purposely designed feature of early keyboards. But after decades of typewriter-design improvement and the eventual move into the computer era, there is no longer a need for a keyboard that purposely slows down the typist.

Some have tried to design other keyboards, such as the Dvorak, which is used by some individuals, but the QWERTY keyboard remains the most common due to **the momentum of history**. Typing teachers teach QWERTY. Every computer company in the world still lays out the keys in the QWERTY formation, and almost nobody bothers to question the system. It's a broken paradigm that's costing individuals and society massive productivity.

Something similar is happening with our aversion to borrowing for investing purposes. Because of the momentum of history and the lack of solid financial education, we remain stuck in the old false belief that borrowing to invest is risky. I'm certain that most people, if they were to truly understand the lost opportunity cost incurred, would change their behaviour.

Short-Term, Impulsive Investing Decisions

Imagine this scenario with me for a moment: Two men walk through the posh downtown streets of a cosmopolitan city. They pass by some ultra-flashy clothing shops and boutique food and wine shops, and eventually they come across a Porsche dealership.

Sitting in the window is a sleek and stylish Porsche 911 Carrera. The car is stunning in its beauty, and the men stumble toward the window, drawn to the car like opinions to Facebook.

One of the men, Joe, says, "I'd love to buy one of those."

His friend, Don, looks at the price tag and says, "It'll cost ya! $102,200. Yikes, that's expensive."

Joe agrees and, grumbling about the cost of it, walks away with his head held low.

The men finish their evening, go home, and don't mention the car again until a year later, when they walk past the exact same dealership again and see the *exact* same car — not the next year's model, but the literal same car. Again they forget about everything else and move toward the window like children toward candy.

Joe remembers how much he loves the car and says, "I'd love to have one of those."

Don, ever the realist, pipes up again. "Hey Joe, check this out. It's not just the same model. It's actually the exact same car as last year, but now the list price is $112,420. Pretty expensive."

"You're right. That's too damned expensive. I love the car, but there is no way I'd ever pay that much money for it," says Joe.

Fast forward another year, and the two men repeat the exact same situation again, but this time the price is $123,662. Yet again Joe dreams of buying the car, but Don points out how bad of a deal the car would be. Joe is starting to see a pattern. To himself he thinks, "Wow, this car just keeps going up in value. If it goes up again next year I'm jumping on it!"

Fast forward one more year, and the two men are once again walking past their favourite Porsche dealership, and sure enough the same car is sitting right there where it's always been. They drool on the window and Joe shouts out, "That's it! Tomorrow morning I'm marching right back in here and buying this car."

Don points out that the car is now listed at $136,028. Joe smiles, knowing that he's about to purchase a great deal.

"Don, you're so silly. If only I would have bought it in the first year. Listening to you was the worst decision I ever made. I have to buy this car before it gets even more expensive."

The next morning, Joe strides cockily into the dealership, strokes out a cheque for the car, and drives off the lot with what he is certain will be not only the most fun he's ever had, but also a great deal. "Imagine how much it would cost the next year," he reasons.

Joe is acting crazy, right? Why would anyone buy a product *only after* the price inflated dramatically? He's been fleeced. The car is a consumer good that we know should go down in value with age — not to mention the value loss Joe will take the moment he drives it off the lot.

Yet this is precisely what retail investors do, year after year. It seems absurd when we overlay the actions of retail investors on top of a traditional retail purchase because we all know that waiting and buying older goods like cars and clothes results in cheaper purchases, not more expensive ones.

The decision to buy this car after year three is no different than the decision to invest money in a mutual fund after it went up by x percent in year one, x percent in year two, and then x percent in year three. In fact, if you check the math, it's the exact same. And in this way we should treat it the same. We should know that we will lose value if we buy at the top of the market.

Of course, investments are different insofar as we reasonably expect the value of an investment to rise over time. Where our mental model fails us is in the way that we perceive the *need* to buy into hot markets — typically near the end of a market run.

It takes great care, focus, and strong mental modelling to overcome our biases. One of the better known is our bias toward social proof. We believe something is real only when it's been proven by a certain number of people across society. Some people require little social proof to make a decision. Others require more, but the best investors don't use any social proof, relying on sound investment principles instead.

Most people aren't great investors, though, and this need for social proof is one of the reasons. Most people wait until it's "common sense" before taking action. But by the time everybody knows about a can't-miss investment, you can bet that it means the investment is overpriced and the market is begging for a correction.

When the correction happens, the last ones to buy into the market lose the most money. Many of these folks who got into the market last then panic and sell their investments out of fear of losing it all. They pull their money out of the market and say, "You can't make money in xyz market."

They pull their investments out of the stock market when there is a big correction, believing the world's gone mad and all of their money is going to disappear forever. Then they decide to go into real estate, buying two properties before encountering their first difficult tenant. Then they sell their real estate holdings, believing that it's impossible to make money in real estate.

The principles are so simple we often don't believe them, so we overthink things and commit the biggest investing sin: impulsiveness. For the principles to work, we need to apply them repeatedly, which sometimes becomes difficult when the market or another facet of the business behaves in a way we don't want. Overcoming the compulsion to run when something doesn't go our way is the true battle. We must create a mental model that works, which means being fully aware of the potential for market disruption. Often the best decision we can make when investing is the decision to do nothing.

Even the last buyer into the stock market in 2008 would have regained their losses by March of 2013 if invested across the Dow Jones Industrial Average, for example.[14] Of course, the last buyer in was most likely the first to sell when the market took a tumble, but the folks who had been in for many years prior likely sold just *before* the tumble. Follow the actions of Warren Buffett and others of his ilk and you will see that they buy when the markets are down and sell when they're high. It sounds so easy, but most retail investors end up doing the opposite.

I urge you strongly to develop the mental fortitude to, first, be highly aware of your investment decisions before making them and, second, be slow to change course. Continue using the same strategy until it provides the result you're looking for. Put the right team in place, someone like me to monitor and advise you on your mortgage, a great financial planner, and a realtor like Simon to advise you on purchasing, holding, and selling real estate investments.

Remember that, in spite of intentions, your subconscious mental models can sabotage your best efforts. Thinking mathematically isn't intuitive, and overcoming the desire to flee a bad situation is often counterintuitive, but these are both exactly what it takes to stay in the market and make thoughtful decisions rather than short-term, impulsive ones.

Misunderstanding How and Why Real Estate Works

Most Canadians watch the value of their homes go up year over year. Sure, there are corrections, but everyone has a story of a parent or grandparent who once purchased a home for an obscenely low price. Simon Giannini, my co-author, tells the story of his parents' first home after moving to Canada. They purchased it for $11,000, and today it's worth well over $500,000.

In strong growth markets across the country, price appreciation like this is the norm, not the outlier. Even for those of us who haven't seen continuous appreciation in our own real estate, most of us watch as our parents retire with their home as their biggest asset. The combination of other retirement savings strategies usually falls well short of the one that wasn't even a retirement strategy — owning a home.

We see this repeatedly, yet we fail to make the connection that purchasing and holding more real estate is the solution to our dreams of a prosperous retirement. Only 3 percent of Canadians invest in real estate outside of their principal residence. Of those 3 percent, a much smaller portion take it far enough, many falling prey to short-term, impulsive decision-making. They don't buy enough to make a difference, or they exit the market too soon.

Real estate wealth creation is a replicable formula. Using sensible leverage and capitalizing on the real estate trifecta of cash flow plus mortgage pay-down plus appreciation, investors consistently earn impressive returns year over year.

We hear horror stories of the dreaded "tenants and toilets," and rather than believing there must be a way to mitigate this risk, we stay away from real estate altogether. Meanwhile, the media goes on producing fantastical stories of a coming collapse. But the economic fundamentals don't and never have supported this theory. Yes, there will always be price corrections, but long-term investors should not be scared by the unpredictable (but expected) behaviour of the markets.

Our failed mental modelling around real estate comes down to these factors: tenant fears, overestimating the difficulty of real estate investing, fear of an impending price collapse, misunderstanding the value of team and knowledge, and analysis paralysis.

I'll discuss each of these factors to clear up the misconceptions. This will mentally prepare you for later in the book, where I discuss how to invest in real estate. Without the correct mental modelling and preparation, many new investors only go through the motions of learning the mechanics. Meanwhile, in their lingering doubt, they carry a perennial "But what about ...?" in their minds. This failed mental model can sabotage new efforts to learn and apply new strategies.

I'm going to ensure these doubts are eradicated in your mind by dealing with the flawed mental models one by one.

Tenant Fears

Many new investors seem to think tenant selection is a random process and that tenant retention is a high-maintenance task. The reality is far different. In truth, tenants don't turn over every year. Many great people with stellar tenant records are perpetual renters or transitional professionals who stay renting for a long period of time.

Furthermore, tenant selection is far from random. The landlord retains a huge amount of control over tenant selection. The mistake new landlords often make is failing to have a correct process. The majority of tenant horror stories come from situations in which the landlord failed to implement the time-tested (but simple) tenant-screening system.

This makes no sense and is a great example of failed mental modelling. It's strange how good, intelligent people can go so far down the road of wealth creation to actually purchase an investment property, and then make the simplest mistake at the most inopportune moment. Tenant selection is utterly vital.

Let's think of it in quantitative terms: When you're renting a $400,000 property to your tenant, it means you're effectively giving them custodial access to a $400,000 asset. Imagine you had $400,000 of your own money invested in GE stock, and at the same time you were in charge of hiring GE's head accountant. Wouldn't it make sense to put together a strong screening process before giving that person access to the books? You would make damn sure your asset was protected.

The example isn't perfect, but it's close enough to make sense. Think of it another way: if you were interviewing an investment advisor for your $400,000 asset, you would do a decent amount of due diligence. Yet people fail to do this when it comes to selecting a tenant, who can do as much or more damage than an unqualified financial advisor.

The great investors who practice the core principles of tenant-selection due diligence soon discover that tenants aren't so bad. They discover that tenant dramas are few and far between and that well-screened tenants are the human resource that ultimately turns those imagined ROIs into real dollars in your bank. When you entrust a tenant to look after a valuable asset, prudent due diligence is merely a cost of entering the arena. It's not a luxury or specialization. Yet many new investors fail to implement this system. We're not talking about a five-interview psychometric test here. We're referring to the basics: rental application, credit check, and background check (calling their past landlords). Visit www.realestateretirementplan.ca to download this checklist, along with several other self-analysis tools.

None of this requires advanced knowledge in property management, just a bit of common sense. And if you hate the idea of doing any of this to avoid major tenant problems later, keep in mind that you don't have to do it yourself. In my own case, I hired a property manager early in my real estate investing career, and I never even meet my tenants. It's not that I don't want to; it's just that I don't have unlimited time, and a property manager can do it better than me. I'm more valuable doing other tasks in the real estate investing business, like analyzing new properties for purchase.

By following a few simple tenant selection principles, you will be able to mitigate the vast majority of the risk in real estate investing. Keep this in mind and don't let the flawed mental model around tenant fears stop you from investing in real estate.

Believing Real Estate Is Only for the Wealthy and Highly Knowledgeable

Immigrating to Canada from Scotland at a young age and being raised by a father who was a ship's captain and a homemaker mother, you might say I became intimately aware of the middle class mindset. Of course, there are many great things about the middle class mindset, but one of them isn't the attitude toward investing. Due to the industrial model of education and the informal education we receive in personal finance, our inherited model says that the middle class works.

We're workers, and workers work.

The middle class doesn't invest in anything, with the possible exception of a plan prepared by our company or through a government-sponsored savings strategy executed by the major banks. I spoke previously about the force of history, which again is at play here in the discussion about the misunderstandings of real estate investment. We don't think of ourselves as investors, because in our minds investors are people with loads of money and loads of specialized knowledge. The underlying assumption is that real estate investing is just something for the wealthy.

This belief is false today, if it was once true. Anyone owning a home with dormant equity can probably access the cash to invest right away. But the bigger issue is the fear of knowledge. Folks think the knowledge required is far more complex than it actually is. I would argue that the barrier to entry in real estate investing is significantly lower than what it would be to manage a stock portfolio. People misunderstand how simple it actually is to invest in real estate.

Yet if you look at the number of people with self-directed stock investments compared to the people with income properties, you'll find that real estate is underrepresented. I see it in my clients all the time. If I look at the people who are brilliant with their own money management, it's a much smaller subset of people than the ones who are multi-millionaires in real estate. I would even argue that the brilliant ones would very likely do much better getting a full-time professional money management team, since this step helps remove the emotional attachment people typically have to their own money.

Some of these fantastic real estate results have to do with leverage and some have to do with the fact that real estate as an asset class has performed well, but I would argue that the largest component is that the barrier to entry in real estate is lower due to less knowledge being required.

You have to know how to sign a purchase and sale agreement, which most people have done already on their own home. You have to be able to calculate basic cash flow, which most people are already capable of doing because of their budget. It's not difficult to decipher whether a property has higher cash flow than expenses. And you have to do a little bit of reading on market dynamics, which isn't as hard as it might seem.

Understanding basic real estate market fundamentals for a major metropolitan city is dramatically easier than understanding the economic fundamentals of a specific asset class within the stock market community. It would be a much more formidable task to deeply understand the merits of investing in precious metals or energy stocks, for example.

Because of this feared knowledge barrier, I've seen too many people throw their arms in the air and fail to invest in real estate. On the other hand, I've also seen hundreds of regular people with normal levels of financial knowledge quickly educate themselves in real estate and, in a relatively short window, create a stable and secure retirement.

I would strongly urge you to educate yourself thoroughly and not be dissuaded by the supposed need for deeply specialized knowledge. You can learn everything you need to know about real estate, and you can do it in a comparatively short period of time.

Fear of an Impending Price Collapse

Every spring in Canada we engage in a made-up event known as RRSP season. Like other made-up events, you can find its source by following the trail of money. What you might not realize about RRSP season is that it's about far more than solid financial planning.

The marketing machine that sells us those fee-heavy investments is firmly at work here. Many prognosticators continually predict the real estate market collapse. But these kinds of predictions are extremely difficult to make. Last I heard there was no legal penalty for making a false prediction. Perhaps if there were we would have a saner society and saner investment behaviour.

Let me state without qualification: any time an asset class over-performs, the probability of a price correction rises. When real estate performs admirably for several years in a row, we must expect a price correction at some point. Every investor must understand this. Temporary setbacks are part of investing. Every investor who's been around for a while will eventually see a price correction. But the prevailing notion of impending real estate doom often bears no resemblance to the real market situation, where corrections combine with consistent growth to form overall performance.

Corrections happen, but remember that in a real estate market (or any market) a drop in value isn't relevant unless you're in a situation in which you need to sell. The only situations in which most of us would need to sell are a negative cash flow situation or a situation in which someone hasn't managed liquidity and needs a cash injection for something else.

When I buy real estate, I'm concerned with cash flow and where I think the value is going to be when I cash in my chips, not where the value will be in the interim. I know that the value will likely fluctuate but that market fundamentals drive the long-term trajectory of the asset — that's where I focus.

Real estate isn't a speculative game. It's a get-rich-slow, buy-and-hold game. All the rules and dynamics outlined in this book are no longer applicable when someone chooses to speculate rather than invest, because speculation is nothing more than gambling. I'm not a proponent of gambling. I'm a proponent of sustainable savings strategies and hedging against inflation to protect retirement incomes and retirement net worth, which is exactly what fundamental real estate investing provides.

Fundamental real estate investing removes the danger of a major impending price collapse because we build the inevitable market fluctuations into our projections and ride through the down times, still earning cash flow on our investments.

There are top economists who have been predicting the collapse in the real estate market since 2005, and they've been getting it wrong since then. If it were easy to time asset classes, then we wouldn't need analysts, investment bankers, investment advisors, and people to go to business school anymore. The economic fundamentals of Canada are complex, but they are only one component of a much larger picture. We now live in an economic environment in which we are hugely affected by global trade, exports, imports, and other less concrete forces. Anyone who believes he or she can time the real estate, stock, or other markets is delusional, lying, or keeping him or herself well hidden.

Predictions of the real estate market collapse are great for selling newspapers and churning up fear in the masses, but there is simply no way of knowing with absolute certainty in advance when a major correction will come.

We don't know the moment when the market will correct. We don't know how major the correction will be. But we do know one thing for certain: that residential real estate isn't going anywhere. I can't say with any certainty whether Google or Apple will be around in ten years, but I can tell you with one hundred percent certainty that in Canada it will get really cold in the winter and people will want housing. It's not an asset class that will disappear. Yes, it's overvalued in a few key markets, and I would recommend not buying there. But as an entire asset class, it will avoid the major price collapse that some predict simply because there will always be a need for it.

If you're investing in major markets, there is no more space to build at the same time as there is a net migration into the cities. Simple supply and demand stipulates that prices will remain robust (taking into account the inevitable corrections) for the foreseeable future.

My advice to new real estate investors is to not get caught up in what's going to happen in the short term. Look at the market fundamentals and analyze with the best knowledge available what the value will be on the day you want to cash in your chips. Thinking of the short term will cause you to make impulsive investment decisions that won't help you in the long term.

Failure to Build a Team

When a client comes to my office looking for a real estate investment mortgage, I take the opportunity to recommend the most trusted members of my team. There are plenty of excellent real estate agents, property managers, and renovators out there, but there are also some bad ones, which is why, if possible, I like to make recommendations to my clients.

However, my clients often choose their own team or go it alone, and sometimes the result is less than ideal. In one circumstance, a client decided to purchase a property without the representation of a real estate agent. This meant, of course, that my client would not get advice on any of the dozens of potential purchase pitfalls. Not knowing any better, he (my client) went ahead with the purchase of the property in spite of some irregularities with the real property report (survey).

The property was a solid investment for a couple of years. However, he then wanted to sell the property in order to consolidate some cash holdings to buy a bigger investment. Believing he had succeeded the first time, my client chose to forego hiring a qualified real estate agent again. When it came time to sell, the buyer's real estate agent was, of course, savvier than my client and took a closer look at the survey.

The experienced agent soon found that the deck on the property had been built without a permit and that the chain link fence encroached on the neighbour's property. The buyer, heeding the advice of her top-notch real estate agent, made an offer on the property conditional to the two problems being fixed at the seller's (my client's) expense.

In the end, my client was forced to spend about $18,000 of the proceeds to fix the problems, and all because he didn't use a great real estate agent when purchasing the property. What should have been a highly profitable real estate deal turned into a pedestrian one simply because my client had one weak link in his team — himself.

The tendency to try to go it alone and do everything ourselves is a major mental modelling flaw when it comes to real estate. It feels like we're saving money by doing it ourselves, but in the long run it usually ends up costing money.

Building real estate as a retirement plan is much like building your RRSP. You need a team. Trying to do it all alone will ensure frustration, and inevitably at some point you will suffer as a result of not taking advantage of professional knowledge.

The good news is that teams of competent real estate people exist in every major (or even just decent-sized) market in Canada. A good team doesn't require a super-sophisticated group of people, but you need a good lender and realtor, and you will probably need a good property manager. You can do the property management yourself, but I wouldn't recommend that beyond the first one or two properties.

There are a couple of reasons for this. First, if you're like me, you're not that impressive with a hammer. A good property manager is someone who can make small repairs on his or her own and can manage a renovation team to do other repairs. If you choose to manage your own properties, it also means maintaining a book of contacts, such as a plumber, an electrician, a painter, and a flooring installer. If you hire a property manager, he or she will maintain that entire Rolodex of contacts on your behalf, plus handle a thousand small problems you truly don't want to touch.

That said, the people with the skillset to manage properties can go ahead and do it themselves if they wish, but please pause and think about the second reason why self-managing is a bad idea: the value of your time. Consider it carefully before taking on the role of property manager. In some circumstances it might be the best use of your time, but in many circumstances it won't be, especially if you're already earning a strong income in a different field. Much property management work is low-wage work, so you will effectively be losing money by spending your time here.

Failure of Education

I had a surreal experience the other day while enjoying a meal in a pub with a couple of friends. These happened to be my two fittest friends, and all three of us considered the pub meal to be an enjoyable part of our "cheat day," when we put aside our regular diet rules and just eat whatever the heck we want.

The indulgence was fun but led to a lengthy discussion about nutrition. Each of these friends is highly knowledgeable about food, and I take much of my fitness and nutritional knowledge directly from them. Both are avid readers on fitness and nutrition, so their opinions are well formed. They also both have six-packs in their forties, which I don't see all that often.

We finished up our conversation and eventually left the pub. On the way out the door I overheard a snippet of conversation coming from another table. This table was also talking about nutrition and fitness in their own way. I heard one of the conversationalists loudly and proudly proclaim, "Yeah, I'm taking care of my fitness a lot more now. I switched from regular to light beer."

The claim jolted me and I jerked my head around to see the speaker. Perhaps unsurprisingly, I saw a man who didn't look healthy at all. In fact, the entire table looked unhealthy. I thought about that moment for quite some time afterwards. The contrast between my super-fit friends and this table really came down to knowledge and self-education.

It's the age-old story: the people who need the information most aren't getting it. The super-fit people share high-level knowledge amongst each other, while unfit people struggle with poor information and knowledge. The same thing happens with financial education. Failing to educate oneself is one of the most insidious mental modelling flaws when it comes to misunderstanding how real estate works. It comes from availability bias, where we simply assume that what's currently available to us is exactly what there is. But the knowledge that we need the most is precisely the knowledge we don't have before us. We must go out in search of it.

Without such knowledge, our investments will suffer. Just as a weak link in your real estate investing team can sabotage your efforts, so can a weak link in your knowledge. As you will remember, I urged you not to believe that real estate investing is solely the domain of the rich and ultra-educated. But I certainly don't want to give you the impression that education is unimportant. It's vital to have a healthy appetite for knowledge when getting into real estate investing. A failure to learn is a failure to grow in all domains. Real estate is no different.

In our office we are blessed to have many clients who take their education very seriously. Regardless of what new clients claim to know, however, we always start each client consultation with the assumption that they need to understand the fundamentals, so part of our client onboarding process is giving out books on the ABCs of real estate investing. We also provide them with the fundamental Excel spreadsheets required to analyze property, as well as articles on screening tenants. Each of these tools can be found at www.realestateretirementplan.ca. If you haven't already done so, please go there now and download the educational and practical tools needed so you can augment your education.

Believe it or not, though, there is another way that people fail when it comes to education. They believe they need a lot more than they actually do. Knowledge is great, but I'm most concerned with having a functional understanding. You don't need to be the best real estate analyst in Canada to build a real estate portfolio that supports your retirement goals. You just need the basics. It's probably not a good use of your time or mental capacity to aim at teaching others to invest in real estate or writing a book on real estate investing.

Analysis Paralysis Around Buying Real Estate

One of the hallmarks of the overly analytical type (the type that are traditionally engineers, finance majors, or lawyers) is a tendency to not take action. I've known many a finance major who could prove unequivocally that a business model will work well past the time when the opportunity has passed. There are so many brilliant MBAs who fail to realize that business doesn't get done on a case study in a textbook.

One example was a client named Mark (not his real name). Mark is a brilliant guy, an MBA who graduated from one of Canada's top schools and became a professional "quants geek." At some point Mark realized that real estate would be a great investment class for his personal finances, and he went all the way into real estate.

But when I say he went all the way into real estate, I mean he spent a lot of time researching real estate. He never actually purchased a property. I knew he was doing a lot of research because he told me about his practice of spending two or three hours most nights working on real estate. When he initially came into my office, I asked him all the normal questions, and we uncovered very quickly that qualifying for the mortgage and raising capital for the purchase wouldn't be a problem at all. Mark was ready to buy within a couple of days.

Then he disappeared. I was shocked when I saw him two years later at a real estate meeting and learned that he hadn't purchased a single property. Nothing was holding Mark back but himself. He wanted to understand the answers to a thousand questions when he only needed the answers to ten. He was overthinking a simple problem.

Once you understand the principles and have completed a thorough but basic analysis, please pull the trigger and purchase the property rather than seeking the answers to 990 more questions than necessary. One thing I can tell you for absolute certain: you don't make money on real estate deals you never do or stocks you never buy.

Tunnel Vision on Paying Off Debt (Even Good Debt)

There was a time when my office had as clients many finance MBAs from the top business schools in Canada, as a by-product of the teaching I did at MBA programs and my network. What stood out even amongst these top young financial minds was the relative lack of personal finance education.

Put more accurately, these people understood the timeless concepts of finance — capital, debt, and borrowing — as they relate to the corporate context, yet they struggled to see how these concepts applied to their own personal finance context. Amongst these MBAs, the most common flaw our office would see regularly was being psychologically attached to paying down student loan debt, even though a) it created a tax deduction, and b) the real cost of borrowing is lower than a mortgage.

We're back to that old canard, "Debt is evil." It's shocking to see this mental modelling flaw manifest itself in these high-level finance thinkers.

Sadly, there are real-world negative consequences to this false belief. Here's what happens: Subconsciously believing debt is evil, people funnel all of their financial resources toward paying down debt. They believe paying down their mortgage is the first principle of personal finance, and a corollary of this belief is that they would never dream of borrowing to invest.

While focused on paying down debt, they fail to invest. This is a problem, because the opportunity cost of waiting to invest is enormous. Compounding power works wonders the earlier it is deployed. People can't even catch up on their RRSP contributions because they've funneled extra cash for years into paying down debt — even tax-deductible debt, which is the best kind.

Make no mistake: paying down high-interest non-deductible debt or debt that could compromise your household's ability to make payments is one of the most important personal finance steps. Credit cards consistently charge above 15 percent. There isn't an investment advisor in the world who could promise you a better after-tax return than that. But having tunnel vision about paying off good, low-interest, tax-deductible debt might be one of the worst mental modelling flaws in our society today.

Making Image-Based Financial Decisions

The finance MBAs, medical professionals, and law school graduates I spoke about previously are particularly prone to this error. One of them (let's call him Ron) was in my office wanting to refinance his home a couple of years ago.

"Perfect, here's a smart young MBA grad who gets it. He's going to apply the timeless principles of investing to his own life," I thought.

But he said, "Real estate values have risen since I bought my home. I think it's time to refinance, pull out some equity, and finally buy my Mercedes S-Class."

I paused. Had I really just heard that? I measured myself before responding, thinking to myself, "'Finally'? He's only twenty-nine."

I knew Ron was about to make one of the cardinal mistakes of youth — spending piles of perfectly good cash on his image when it would serve no good purpose and steal from his future. Worse still, when someone decides to debt-finance his or her image, it's usually the harbinger of future poor image-based financial decisions.

I could already see Ron's future. He would be in my office in another couple years when his home appreciated some more, this time to purchase a boat, and then a cottage, and on it goes. Cheap consumer debt is like a bad virus when it could be such a great tool.

After considering how to respond, I tried my best to convince him to seek the advice of a top financial planner before making this decision. I explained the merits of real estate investing.

"Oh yes, I definitely plan on investing in real estate, but first I need to get this car. It's important for my career."

I've seen many intelligent professionals contort the truth like this. They believe that they must invest heavily in their image in order to develop future success, like somehow driving a Mercedes instead of a Toyota is the secret key to career development. Not hard work. Not continuous professional development. Not working on communication skills like writing or speaking. It's the car that makes the difference in one's career.

I didn't get through to Ron. He financed the purchase of his $80,000 car instead. This was about five years ago, which means that even though I know nothing else about Ron, I know that he's about $150,000 poorer as a result of that single decision. Instead of using the $80,000 for a down payment on a real estate asset (that would have appreciated at least $100,000 since then), he lost the bulk of the value on his car.

Cars depreciate fast. Even fancy cars. Real estate tends to appreciate. And because he used the debt for an image-based purchase, he was unable to deduct the interest from his taxes. It was a costly decision for Ron.

When you add a few choices of this type together, you end up far behind the game. Sadly, Ron's choice isn't an uncommon one. Because of this mental modelling flaw and the others I've discussed, there is a large sector of our society without secure, stable retirements. This is why many are being forced to consider lowering their quality of life during retirement. Many are forced to downsize their home, and, worse still, others are taking on low-paying labour to make up the shortfall between their income and expenses.

SELF-ASSESS YOUR FINANCIAL MENTAL MODELS

Spend some time answering the following questions. Based on your answers, do you think you are at risk of personal finance self-sabotage? It's only by examining our beliefs that we can improve them and overcome the false financial paradigms of our own families or society as a whole.

- Do you believe that all debt is "evil"?
- Do you think borrowing to invest is too risky?
- Do you truly understand how and why real estate investing works?
- Do you think tenants and property management are likely to destroy any returns you might gain from real estate investing?
- Do you think you have to invest in real estate all on your own, without a team?
- Do you think the education and cash barrier to investing in real estate is too high to pass?
- Do you wait until it's obvious to everyone that a market is making money before investing in it?
- Has your investment account suffered because you've failed to invest until after paying off all debt?
- Have you made image-based purchases with either debt financing or cash?
- If so, how much has it set back your future?

SCRUB YOUR MIND OF FALSE MODELS

Being the owner of a bad financial mental model or two is nothing to be ashamed of. Financial thinking doesn't lend itself well to intuition, and our society doesn't educate us to succeed financially.

The fact that you are reading this book is a great sign. You're well on your way to overcoming any poor mental models you might have. The best way to scrub your mind of these beliefs is simply to examine your thinking whenever dealing with a personal finance issue. Double check and examine your thoughts. Then spend more time educating yourself. If you don't believe in the benefits of borrowing to invest, for example, learn more until the truth becomes painfully obvious.

The rest of this book will take you a long way toward understanding the enormous financial benefit of borrowing money to invest. The same can be said about the other poor mental modelling patterns discussed. But I would urge you to continue your education beyond this book.

CHAPTER 4
The Portfolio Approach to Real Estate

Owning a variety of asset classes means that some part of your portfolio
will be doing well when the cyclical turmoil arises. A broadly diversified portfolio includes large capitalization stocks, small cap, emerging
markets, fixed income, real estate and commodities.

— BARRY RITHOLTZ

It's an unfortunate state of affairs in the personal finance world when
many Canadians have good reason not to trust their financial planners
and advisors. I've tried to illustrate how the longstanding system managed
by the big banks no longer serves the individual investor and prospective
retiree, if in fact it ever did.

Good folks, seeking stable and secure retirements, have followed the
same path for decades. They trust the advice of their advisor and put their
money into the same mutual funds as everyone else. The banks get rich
and the "advisor" often earns a commission.

Later in this chapter, I'll show you how to select a financial planner
whose interests are aligned with yours. But for now just let me say that
the first criterion of selecting the right financial planner is to avoid at all
cost those whose income is derived from commissions. There are many
problems with this type of arrangement, and amongst the most egregious
is the fact that commission-based financial planners and advisors never
council their clients to invest in private real estate.

Why would they when they can't earn a commission?

Of course, you will have to pay for top-notch financial planning services. But it's worth it. Understanding and executing a full-blown financial plan takes more expertise than most folks can muster at their current level of knowledge. When paying for anything, it's nice to know that your service provider's interests are aligned with your own.

No truly professional financial planner would advise against real estate entirely. It's far too important of an asset class to avoid. Deciding upon the weight given to real estate in an individual's portfolio is a highly detailed task. Balancing such a portfolio is what we pay financial advisors to do. But almost without qualification, I would say that every portfolio should include at least some component of real estate.

But what do I know? For your own education, it's nice to know what an experienced and accredited financial planner like me is saying, but it's also nice to say, "Look at what all the large pension funds are doing." They always have a solid asset allocation in real estate, and if they are Canadian-based, it's Canadian-based real estate. These pension fund managers are probably the smartest tier of investors in the entire country. You can look at the CPP fund managers or the Alberta pension fund, for example, and they always have at least 20 percent — but usually 30 to 35 percent — in real estate.

That tells me something. I always believe in watching how the top people act — following the smart money — because by watching the financial wizards of the world, we can see how they treat both real estate and the use of debt capital for investing.

The combined power of borrowing to invest and allocating a significant portion of your portfolio to real estate is an important driver in your ability to create wealth. I'll make the case for why and how real estate fits into an overall investment approach and financial plan. I'll also give you the financial planning perspective on borrowing to invest.

Borrowing to invest in real estate is a great basic strategy, but without a solid financial plan, investors are far more likely to make critical mistakes in each of these areas. It's important to invest in real estate, but it's more important to build an entire portfolio of investments that will support you through all types of markets, maximizing gains while still minimizing risks.

I'll first discuss why real estate is important as part of a portfolio and how to make sure you're doing it right. Next, we'll move onto a discussion of borrowing to invest and how to make sure you're doing that right too. Finally, we'll end with a discussion on selecting a financial planner.

HOW REAL ESTATE FITS INTO YOUR OVERALL PORTFOLIO

I'm a big believer in real estate, so long as it's one part of an overall financial plan. From a financial planning perspective, there are several reasons to include real estate in your portfolio. But before I dive into those, I would like to present a caveat: the vast majority of individual investors would benefit mightily by getting the advice and guidance of professional financial planning services. Books like this are incredibly powerful for opening readers' eyes to financial possibilities, but I liken personal finance to medicine. Sure, you can read about certain health conditions and the cures for them, but do you really want to try curing them on your own?

A great financial plan takes everything into consideration — your goals, your current income, your desired future income, your time horizon, and many more factors. A great financial planner will plug all of these factors into a large matrix and help you arrive at a specific plan that minimizes risk while maximizing returns. In addition, this kind of financial planner will also take into account succession planning and tax strategy. They will be able to deliver all of this under the same roof with all the relevant professionals. The combined effect of each of these services is enormously powerful.

Please don't go it alone. Find a great financial planner and use their services. Later in this chapter I've included a section on how to identify such a financial planner. But one of the indicators you've found a great financial planner is that they won't shy away from real estate. Contrast that with a certain type of financial advisor who historically said that real estate wasn't a secure or profitable investment.

This was a great lie. In truth, there was only one reason for the perpetuation of this lie: they weren't able to profit from clients' real estate investments, so they steered folks away from it. They received commissions for selling certain mutual funds, and thus they told their clients for years that mutual funds were really the only type of investment to make.

This has led to many poor financial decisions. Potentially millions of Canadians who should have invested in real estate haven't. It's a shame, because there are many benefits. Let's take a look at them one by one.

Less Volatility

One common experience shared by a large cohort of society is having experienced less volatility when invested in real estate instead of just stocks and bonds. Much of that has to do with the fact that once you invest in real estate, nobody values that real estate daily or sends you a monthly statement on the market fluctuations of your property. If people could log in online and see the value of their homes going up and down daily, I think they would buy and sell more quickly, as they do with stocks — especially if they could sell it and get the money in three days, as you can in the stock market.

Imagine a world where people day-trade houses. It would force the rise of a whole new class of real estate analysis. I would not want that to happen because, while the stock market is great in many ways, the lack of liquidity provided by real estate is actually a good thing. The lack of transparency over the absolute current market value works in individual investors' favours. When people have a low tolerance for risk, the real estate market often provides them with a safe haven because of the reduced volatility caused by lack of liquidity.

Diversification

The lack of liquidity is a major hedge against volatility, but another big part is diversification. If you are a Canadian real estate investor, you would have fared extremely well in 2008 compared to the average investor who was just in stocks and bonds, whether through mutual funds or in individual stocks and bonds. Those investors' portfolios dropped precipitously, certainly much more than did the portfolios of those who had 20 or 30 percent in real estate investments.

The same could be said in reverse, of course, if the real estate market ever takes a huge tumble as the stock market did in 2008. Then it becomes all the more important to be diversified. It's always good to be invested in an asset class that's not correlated to the broad stock market and that also delivers strong rates of returns.

In the financial planning world there is a concept known as the Markowitz Efficient Frontier (or just the Efficient Frontier). The point of this measure is to be very clear about the level of risk acceptable for the expected return. If you can get the same return for lower risk, you should always weight your portfolio that way. It shows the set of optimal portfolios balancing acceptable risk with expected return. If a portfolio is below the Efficient Frontier, it's a sign of a sub-optimal portfolio — too low of a return for the risk level. Diversification has shown to improve optimization of portfolios. In other words, diversified portfolios strike the correct balance between risk and expected return. On the other side, sub-optimal portfolios are typically less diversified.[15] This is a key, basic component of financial planning.

You can't consider your investment portfolio truly and properly diversified without including real estate. The optimal amount of real estate in your portfolio will depend on your specific circumstances and goals, but one thing is certain: real estate should always play a role.

Tax Savings

Real estate provides the opportunity not only to make a great rate of return, but also to earn a great after-tax rate of return by virtue of all the tax strategies that you can employ when investing in real estate.

First, a significant portion of the earnings from any real estate investment will be taxed as capital gains. Since only half of capital gains are taxed, you end up paying significantly less tax than you would on normal income. And of course you only pay those capital gains when selling, which means you defer payment until a later date. Deferment is second only to not paying taxes in its power.

Second, you create a tax deduction by borrowing to invest. The mortgage you take out on any investment property will automatically create a significant tax deduction. This means the after-tax cost of borrowing is minimized.

Rate of Return

If you look at any historical statistics, you'll see that the all-in rates of return have certainly been above average — and at least in line with — stock market rates of return. With rates of return that strong, and after throwing in the other benefits of real estate, it truly begins to make sense.

In fact, one of the longest-standing criticisms of real estate investing has been the lower rates of return compared to the stock market over the long term. But that's just not what we're seeing. Plus, most of these critics only consider appreciation in their return calculations. They typically don't take into account the forced savings mechanism of principal pay-down or the cash flow that a property can generate. When you factor those in, real estate typically earns as much as the stock market and often more.

Protection of Principal

I always ask clients, "Have you ever heard of someone who has lost money investing in stocks?" Everyone has heard of somebody, usually including him or herself. But when I ask, "Have you ever heard of someone losing money in real estate?" they often have a very hard time thinking of anyone. Most of my clients don't know a single person who has lost money in real estate in a long-term hold cycle. Please note: I'm not saying folks don't lose money in real estate. Of course they do, but it's far less common than losing money in the stock market, and when it does happen, it's typically the result of panicked selling.

It's very hard. You've got to really screw up to lose money in real estate. Part of it comes down to that lack of liquidity. You might want to sell, but by the time you get the sign on the front lawn, things may have changed. Maybe nobody wants to buy it at your price, so you wait, realizing you haven't lost any money until you sell. Then, two years later, when you get around to considering a sale again, you find the market has recovered.

Investors rarely lose their principal, which makes real estate a great choice.

Hedge Against Inflation

In an inflationary environment, there is nothing riskier than being heavily weighted in cash. Since real estate is valued in the currency that's inflating, you can trust that at the very least it won't lose value due to inflation. But income properties offer a further hedge against inflation because they earn income. The landlord has a measure of control over the amount of rent collected, which can rise along with inflation. At the very least, with the rise in property value and rents collected, the investor ends up keeping pace with inflation.

Monthly Coupon

Real estate investments, when done right, can essentially replace (or seriously buttress) a pension. Some real estate investments are stronger on cash flow than others. Investors moving toward the end of their financial horizon can strategically position their portfolios for more cash flow. This cash flow, which is distributed monthly in the form of rental income, is often the perfect pension replacement.

DRAWBACKS OF NOT INVESTING IN REAL ESTATE

I like to think of problems from both sides. We just looked at the benefits. Now let's look at the drawbacks of not investing in real estate.

It's quite simple: the drawbacks are simply the inverse of all the benefits we just discussed.

Without real estate, you'll be less diversified, so rates of return will be more volatile. Think back to the subprime crisis. Being invested in Canadian real estate certainly would have been good at that time. Without real estate, you won't have the same protection of principal, let alone a solid rate of return.

Without real estate, you lose its tax benefits. You will still benefit from capital gains with other investment classes, but the borrowing-to-invest tax deductions, which are commonplace when investing in real estate, are less common when investing in other asset classes.

Without real estate investments, your rates of return will be limited to what the stock and bond markets provide. This is a problem, since these days the bond market is earning only 1 or 2 percent. The stock market can earn a strong return (often 8 to 11 percent), but these returns are often choppy. Investing in the stock market, you will go through periods like 2008, when markets were down 45 percent. If you limit yourself, it will mean missing out on the massive benefits of real estate while exposing yourself to more risk.

Not investing in real estate is like not investing in other nations' stock markets. Why, if you had the choice, would you only invest in Canadian stocks? Why wouldn't you buy U.S. or European stocks? It's a form of investment self-sabotage whenever you limit yourself or exclude a large, well-known, well-established asset class such as Canadian real estate.

WHO IS REAL ESTATE FOR?

Private real estate is a powerful asset class that everyone should have access to, but the ability of an individual (or couple) to purchase individual real estate properties often comes down to the size of their starting portfolio. Some individuals don't have large enough starting portfolios to justify purchasing private real estate. No matter; if you're trusting your money to a great financial planner, he or she will make sure that you're invested in real estate via other means, like real estate investment trusts (REITs).

Still, there is a benefit to private real estate investments like rental properties, just as with individual stocks versus mutual funds. Whether as part of a mutual fund or in an individual stock, both are stock market investments. Either way, it's a great asset class. Mutual funds work better for someone with a small starting portfolio, but for someone with a larger starting portfolio, it probably makes sense to purchase individual stocks. It really just depends on what stage of life you're at and the size of your portfolio.

The same could be said for real estate. If you've got enough money to buy private rental properties, it's a great idea. I'll discuss the issue of how to allocate borrowed money in the next section of this chapter.

But outside the issue of access to funds, time horizon is a major consideration when considering where in a portfolio real estate fits. At the very minimum, you have to give a real estate investment five years for profitability, and a better time horizon is probably ten years. If you need that liquidity in three or four years, you might be better off weighting your portfolio less on the real estate side. As always, consult with your financial planner.

Additionally, to mitigate risk, you need to ensure that your household income could support you in the event of lost rental income. As Simon will discuss later in the real estate section, you will want to account for the odd vacancy when analyzing rental properties. The idea is to put aside the money for lost income in advance, but until your real estate portfolio is large enough to cover off the odd vacancy with overall cash, it's a good idea to make sure your household income would be enough in case of emergency.

You'll also want to consider the size of your initial capital, which is spread across what you currently have in cash, savings, and investment accounts, and what you can access from your real estate equity.

You may also have some specific retirement goals or other financial goals, which would be important to consider. Do you want to live abroad? Will you need a monthly coupon? Are you looking to pass along wealth to your children or grandchildren? These and many more potential questions may affect your plans to invest in real estate.

Finally, you will want to consider your liquidity. Real estate is highly illiquid. This is actually a really good thing because it forces us to sit through small market hiccups, but it's vital we plan for this lack of liquidity. If we foresee needing a large chunk of cash in short order, then it's important to weight your portfolio less heavily in real estate.

BORROWING TO INVEST WITH A PORTFOLIO APPROACH

As I've emphasized, borrowing to invest can be immensely powerful. But even in circumstances in which the debt capital deployed comes from dormant home equity, investors should take an overall portfolio approach. People often seem to think that if they borrow from their home equity, they should use that money to invest in real estate. This is false.

I always look at it from a holistic approach. I agree that individuals should access that money because it's cheap — cheaper once the tax deduction is applied to arrive at the after-tax cost of borrowing. But if 30 percent of your capital should be allocated to real estate, then it means 30 percent of that borrowed money should also go toward real estate.

If the dormant equity is a small amount, then the chance you'll be able to buy a private real estate investment is reduced. To ensure you have a well-balanced portfolio, don't cash in all your other investments to fund one real estate investment. Your financial planner will help you achieve a balanced portfolio, even if you can't buy private real estate, by offering some stellar passive real estate investments, whether public REITs, private REITs, or other types.

The point is to not go all in on real estate just because you have a chunk of dormant equity available. It's vital to take a portfolio approach. But many thousands, and possibly millions, of Canadians have a significant enough chunk of dormant equity that they can purchase a private real estate investment with it and then use the rest of the borrowed funds to invest elsewhere. Remember that all investments using borrowed money create a tax deduction, not just those in real estate. As long as your risk tolerance allows for it, you should probably access that cheap money, but also stick with the optimal asset allocation designed specifically for you.

But before you ever consider borrowing to invest, invest all of your savings (RRSPs, TFSAs, RESPs, and other non-RRSP savings). The goal is that none of your money sits dormant in a bank account earning nothing. That's the first step.

In addition to that, you may have money by way of equity in real estate that you can access. This is a particularly good deal when you factor in today's miniscule cost of capital (the interest rate), but it will likely remain a good deal even when interest rates go up — so long as tax laws remain the same — because the cost to borrow is significantly mitigated by the tax deduction it creates.

So long as borrowed funds earn a greater after-tax rate of return than the after-tax cost of borrowing, it's a wise idea to borrow to invest. You're earning a spread on the borrowed money. It's like having a money factory. An individual's investment capital is made up of what you have *plus* what you have access to at very low borrowing rates.

Then it becomes a question of how to best invest the capital available. Whether it's investing in private real estate, bonds, stocks, or mutual funds, you should be using the services of a professional financial planner for advice. Any professional financial planner worth his or her salt will advise you to have a balanced portfolio, whether borrowing the money to invest or using your own capital. Today's financial planner should be able to give you advice across all major asset classes, but the average financial advisor doesn't do that. It wasn't that long ago that you would need a specialist stockbroker and bond broker. Now you go to one person for anything public, but I think more and more financial advisors will start offering a totally holistic approach. They will be able to advise even on private and public real estate. The best offices are already doing that. More will follow because it simply doesn't make sense for folks to avoid an entire asset class simply because their advisor doesn't profit from it.

Find the right financial planner to help you understand the optimal asset allocation for you and make sure that they're including real estate, even if it's private real estate that they can't profit from.

The Proper Use of Debt to Invest

Many people have the goal of completely paying off their home, but it's often a mistake. Having tunnel vision about paying off debt can mean having far less money in the market and not taking advantage of a powerful tax deduction. But the goal of paying off a mortgage has a strong core idea — financial stability. The goal perhaps shouldn't be to pay off the $1 million mortgage, but to have $1 million in equity.

In truth, most individuals would be better off seeking that goal by using borrowed funds to invest in additional real estate and other types of investments. We'll reach the target faster by borrowing to invest and, in the end, if we do it right, we'll have a healthy and diversified portfolio of productive assets rather than a single house that can only produce wealth when we sell it.

Having equity is a good goal, but once you have equity, you don't need to let it sit there. You can further optimize it by borrowing and investing across the optimal asset allocation.

How to Think About Investment Debt

Most Canadians would agree that the Royal Bank is about the safest investment in the country. So it makes sense to look at how the bank allocates and deploys capital. In fact, they do it the same way as pretty much any large, blue chip company.

When you think of the Royal Bank, you probably think it is going to be around forever. So it follows that they must be completely debt-free, right? Wrong. The bank carries debt and it will never pay it off completely.

Sure, it will always have a lot of equity. But it also has a lot of debt. This is what large, stable companies do, and they do it for a reason. They know how to optimize their balance sheets. It comes down to being able to deploy capital. We should follow the lead of the smartest investors on earth. Take a look at how these large corporations manage their own money and you'll find there's not one that doesn't have debt outstanding.

Why You (Perhaps) Shouldn't Borrow to Invest

As powerful as this strategy is, there is no doubt that it's not going to be for everyone.

International stocks are not for everyone. Even real estate isn't for everyone. Borrowing to invest isn't for everyone. From a certain perspective, borrowing to invest presents more risk. Of course, it's not as risky as using borrowed funds to buy liabilities, but there is a risk of loss with every investment, which is magnified when using borrowed funds.

If your need for liquidity is high, if due to your age you have a short time horizon, or if you have a very low tolerance for risk, then you should strongly consider not borrowing to invest. Of course, there is a cost to that as well. It means in all likelihood that you'll be investing only a small chunk of money, which may or may not get you the retirement result you want. But if the emotional cost of borrowing to invest would put you in an insane asylum, then it's probably best to steer clear of this strategy.

SELECTING A FINANCIAL PLANNER

It's vital that all your financial efforts are going in the same direction. There's no point jumping on the borrow-to-invest and real-estate-investing bandwagons unless those efforts are in line with your overall financial plan and goals. The point of this book and the reality is that many (if not most) Canadians of a certain age would benefit dramatically from both borrowing to invest and investing in real estate. You can't know anything for certain, though, without first understanding your own financial goals and then building a plan to get there.

You'll need an excellent financial planner to help you do that. The following are the criteria you should use to select such a planner — one who understands how to help you achieve your goals and will be able to advise on *all* the tools available to you.

Years of Experience

When selecting a financial planner, you want someone with at least seven years of experience. If you think about it, it's kind of like getting a doctor. Do you want a doctor who has never seen a patient before?

Now, a doctor with one year of experience actually isn't that bad because you know they've already done the internship. They've gone through countless years of studying already. But a financial advisor in their first year could be incredibly inexperienced. All you know about them is that they've done a couple of weekends of courses. That doesn't say much.

If they've been in the business for at least seven years, it means they've likely seen at least one full market cycle. This is important, because nothing in this business is a more potent trainer than real-life experience. Take my go-to financial planner, for example. He started financial planning in 1998. This means he's seen the tech bubble, the chaos of 9/11, and the U.S. recession of 2008 — plenty of cycles.

There's nothing like the truth of real experience to help an upstart become a prudent financial planner. Even though we're supposed to be very logical and thoughtful, I've seen too many financial planners get swept away by irrational exuberance and fail to adhere to the quality control procedures of sound financial planning. Experience usually solves this.

Accreditation

I would never hire a financial planner who didn't have at least one recognizable financial planning accreditation and one recognizable investment management accreditation. Seeing that accreditation will tell you that they know how to analyze from both a financial planning perspective and an investment perspective.

Compensation

Always know in advance how your financial planner is being paid. If you're not paying them, you have to ask yourself who is.

Never select a financial planner who is paid by commission for anything to do with stocks, bonds, or mutual funds. The reason is simple: the only way you can be certain that a planner's interests are aligned with yours is if he or she benefits from your investments doing well. In a commission structure, planners make money regardless of how well you're doing on your investments.

Great financial planners only charge their clients a fee for money managed. If their clients earn a strong return after paying their fees and they keep coming back, it means they're happy. Most do.

Most commission-based "financial planners" simply don't get the results. One reason is the erosion of profit from all the various fees their clients pay on investment products purchased. In today's age, there is nothing in the client's best interest that comes out of commissions. Every stock, bond, or mutual fund product available only by commission has an alternative that a fee-based financial planner would have access to. It's only difficult to avoid commission-based sales on insurance and private real estate purchases. In these realms, there often isn't a legitimate fee-based alternative. But when selecting a financial planner, always steer clear of those selling commission-based investments in stocks, bonds, and mutual funds.

Philosophy or Approach

Every financial planner says they are holistic, but it's often not the case. This fact truly manifests itself in the guidance they provide about real estate. To understand the whole picture, they must understand real estate, but often they just ignore the entire asset class.

It makes no sense because real estate is most people's largest asset. If you have a financial advisor who can only look at stocks, bonds, and insurance but can't advise you on real estate, it means you're working with someone who has a real handicap. Worse yet, it might mean you're working with someone who only wants to make money off you from his or her advice.

Sadly, this second case is probably more likely. Unscrupulous financial advisors can't make money off of your real estate, so they'll tell you not to invest in it. Run for the hills if you see this in a financial planner.

Scope of Services

Financial planning and investment advice are critical, but you also want a professional who can help you with will and estate planning. They should have a lawyer on site or at least have a very close relationship with a great lawyer they can recommend.

A full suite of services means they should be able to help you with will preparation for you and your family, insurance planning, and tax preparation. It doesn't make sense to go to one person for tax preparation, another for investment management, and another for estate planning. It should all be handled in-house. In my financial planner's practice, where I'm a client, I've seen the massive service advantage of doing it this way. For example, when his in-house accountant needs information about me he has immediate access to it all under the same roof. Many important financial details are often missed in the back-and-forth between client and professional. Keeping all the financial information where the professionals reside simplifies everything.

But the major monetary benefit happens when your team is working together and your team members are able to talk to each other in order to come up with ideas to further optimize your financial situation. For example, an in-house tax accountant might notice you could benefit from a tax deduction. They would share that with your financial planner, who could then discuss it with you and chat about the merits of borrowing to invest. You might end up heeding this advice and borrow money to invest, thereby creating a tax deduction and in the end saving tens of thousands of dollars. Individual professionals working in their own silos often miss those kinds of details because they have no contact with the rest of your team.

PLANNING PRECEDES SUCCESSFUL ACTION

In this chapter I've attempted to demonstrate how borrowing to invest and making real estate investments might fit into an overall portfolio to give you the best possible chance for a great retirement.

The biggest hole in most real estate books is their unmitigated passion for real estate and their tendency to sell the dream of getting rich quick. I want you to take an alternative path. Yes, I firmly believe in real estate, but I urge you to remember that real estate is just one part of a successful financial plan. I hope you can see how both borrowing to invest and investing in real estate should fit into your overall financial plan.

Perhaps most importantly, I want to arm you with the tools to be able to assess the value of a financial planner. Securing a great planner is the first step to take before seeking mortgage advice, and before looking at properties.

PART 2

The Power of Borrowing to Invest

CHAPTER 5
How Businesses, Investment Firms, Banks, and Entrepreneurs Think About Capital, Investing, and Wealth Creation

> A man who is without capital, and who, by prohibitions upon banking, is practically forbidden to hire any, is in a condition elevated but one degree above that of a chattel slave. He may live; but he can live only as the servant of others; compelled to perform such labor, and to perform it at such prices, as they may see fit to dictate.
>
> — LYSANDER SPOONER

CAPITAL ISN'T THE SAME THING AS MONEY

Here's a nice piece of trivia for you: the word capital is derived from the Latin word *caput*, which means head, as in a head of cattle. Back in the Roman days, a head of cattle was a common asset and form of payment.

Luckily we've come a long way since Roman times, but the word capital has retained some of its meaning from that time. Most people don't think about the fine differences between a word like capital and our common concept of money, but the distinction is an important one because most individuals could stand to gain tremendously from knowing the difference. I believe that if everyone understood this we would begin thinking about capital (particularly financial capital) and wealth creation much differently.

So what is the difference?

Capital is an asset that is deployed in the production of further wealth. In other words, your groceries aren't capital, and your car isn't capital unless you're an Uber driver. Cash in your pocket has the potential to be capital, but only if you deploy it in the production of further wealth. If you owned a factory, the tools would be considered capital since they would be used in the production of further wealth.

But I want to focus mostly on financial capital — in other words, money that is used to produce further wealth. Access to some form of financial capital, debt or equity, is the most valuable tool we can have as wealth creators. When financial capital is deployed intelligently, we grow more wealth and — in the case of consumers seeking to build a safe, secure retirement — hold enough wealth to use in our later years, when we won't be producing as much income.

Building wealth is simple, but because of human nature and poor financial education, it isn't always easy. The most highly trained professionals have, through education and training, overcome the human intuitions that destroy wealth. The masters of capital use the same practices over and over again: employing capital to its highest and best use, staying invested, only calculating the after-tax cost of borrowing and the after-tax rate of return, and using the time value of money in their favour. Successful businesses and investments require capital. With solid research, training, and expertise, the captains of industry deploy cash with the reasonable expectation that they will be rewarded with a return on investment.

There are two types of capital: debt and equity. Both are deployed consistently by businesses toward the purpose of growth. No major success in the economic world takes place without deploying both types of capital. But when it comes to our personal finances, most individuals fail to intelligently use debt to create wealth. This is the major difference between personal-finance actions and the financial wizardry top minds apply to their firms. Now, it would be easy to believe this discrepancy is a result of differing access to financial tools, but this is a (mostly) false belief. Sure, the captains of commerce and the financial wizards of Bay Street and Wall Street create certain complex debt products that individuals can't, but consumers now have access to powerful debt products, specifically mortgages, that they can use to invest and build personal wealth.

By failing to deploy debt capital early in the financial cycle of their lives, consumers miss benefitting from the time value of money. Borrowing money, then earning a spread on that money for many years, is immensely powerful. Cash is always in short supply. It's a universal rule of capital, and most people never create the retirement of their dreams because they simply can't hoard enough cash to fund investments. Thus we must deploy debt capital to grow our personal wealth in the same way that the big minds of the financial world do for corporations. Getting more capital into the market sooner enables us to take advantage of the time value of money. We'll dive into explanations that show how the time value of money works, and we'll demonstrate the difference between a portfolio that takes advantage of the time value of money versus one that doesn't. We'll also talk about how real estate might be the best tool to access this principle.

Financial experts, especially those in real estate, also deploy a concept known as the highest and best use of capital. Simply put, investors attempt to use the capital available to them in the most profitable way possible. For consumers worried about their personal finance, this means, in practical terms, that if you can take $200,000 worth of dormant home equity and spin it into $1 million worth of cash-producing, appreciating real estate assets, you should do so. Allowing the $200,000 to sit dormant is the worst possible use of capital there is. Putting it to work in the real estate market and multiplying the amount of capital at work by five is most often the highest and best use available. But millions of Canadians find themselves with dormant equity. Their balance sheet is full of the laziest money you could imagine.

Finally, financial experts think sophisticatedly about the cost of borrowing and rates of return. Specifically, they ignore both the cost of borrowing before calculating tax and the rate of return before calculating tax. The true cost of borrowing is the cost after taxes have been deducted. It seems to me that many individuals don't understand the true impact tax deductions have when borrowing to invest in real estate. In Ontario, for example, you are at a marginal tax rate of over 33 percent by the time you earn over $45,000 per year. This means that if you borrow at 10 percent, then your after-tax cost of borrowing is less than 7 percent (10 percent × (1−0.33) = 6.7 percent).

Every leveraged real estate investor benefits from tax deductions because their (typically) 80 percent loan-to-value mortgage is tax deductible. However, the investor who also turns dormant home equity into a source of down payments also benefits further by creating a tax deduction where there wasn't one before. We always try to funnel as much money away from the government toward our own purposes as legally possible.

As for rate of return — financial experts never think in terms of pre-tax. They know that all returns will be minimized by taxes, and thus calculate only their after-tax rate of return when making projections.

THE USE OF CAPITAL

Capital can mean many different things, but the most common use for the term is the use we'll focus on here, which could more accurately be called "financial capital," a necessity for getting a business off the ground. It comes from only two sources: debt and equity. Debt is borrowed (bank loans, personal loans, etc.) and must be repaid later with interest. Equity comes from issuing stock in a company and must provide a return.[16]

Of course, when it comes to personal finance, some of the terminology and purposes are slightly different. You wouldn't generate funds by sale of stock. But you could, nevertheless, generate equity capital by selling all or part of your home to another investor.

The point remains: the difference between debt capital and equity capital is a useful distinction for individuals to apply in their personal financial lives, just as it is for investors in businesses. As discussed in the previous chapter, most of us seem to have trouble crossing the mental hurdle of using debt capital as a source of investment funds. But, like the good consumers we are, many of us don't have an issue with using debt to purchase a liability. Instead, we need to think about what the capital can produce in terms of an investment return, rather than what it can do for our ego by being used to purchase a pretty toy. This is exactly how financial experts think about capital. They seek to deploy it in such a way as to earn a return on investment, regardless of whether the source of capital is debt or equity.

To drive this point home, imagine two individuals owning an investment firm. Just to be cheeky, let's call them Muffett and Bunger (rather than Buffett and Munger of Berkshire Hathaway fame), who are two successful old ladies who spend their days analyzing investment opportunities. Every day, a flood of opportunities comes across their desks, but Muffett and Bunger only invest in the best deals they can find because, in addition to simply making profit for their firm, Muffett and Bunger also follow the rule of finding the highest and best use of capital.

One day they stumble across an opportunity to purchase a pharmaceutical company called DrugMeUp. They do a detailed analysis of the market, cash flow, assets, earnings per share, and a thousand other financial gauges. After their analyses, they believe that, to the best of their knowledge, this pharmaceutical company will return 19 percent of its total value per year. That's a pretty good deal, and they just so happen to have that amount of cash in the bank. They decide to buy.

But, while they're putting together the deal to buy DrugMeUp, they come across another deal. This second deal is for an insurance company called JustInCase. Again, they do detailed financial analyses of several factors. After their research, they reckon JustInCase would earn them 20 percent.

As luck would have it (for calculation purposes), they could purchase each company for the same price: $10 million. Muffett and Bunger are financial geniuses, but you don't have to be to know that 20 percent of $10 million ($2 million) is more than 19 percent of $10 million ($1.9 million). So it stands to reason that they would purchase JustInCase, right?

Likely. These returns are outstanding, and they're seeking to take advantage of the highest and best use of capital. But chances are Muffett and Bunger would opt for the third possibility. They would probably buy both, which is an even higher and better use of capital than simply buying one.

Now, remember that they have just enough cash in the bank to buy one of the businesses. They could earn a 20 percent return on JustInCase and a 19 percent return on DrugMeUp, but if they limit themselves to only the cash they have in the bank, they would earn a maximum total return of only $2 million, since they could only buy one of the businesses.

But Muffett and Bunger are savvy investors. They studied finance at top universities, and they know that there are other ways to access and deploy financial capital than by just using what they have in the bank — equity capital. They know that by borrowing money from someone else — debt capital — they can buy both businesses and reap the benefits of buying both. They start to look at the options and learn that they will be able to borrow 100 percent of the value of DrugMeUp. But the lender's goal isn't just to help capitalists like Muffett and Bunger. The lender wants to earn a return in exchange for the risk of lending the money, so they offer a loan of $10 million with a 7 percent interest rate.

Muffett and Bunger hate spending money on anything, so they go back to their office and analyze the loan. They already know (as much as they're able) that DrugMeUp will return 19 percent of its value back each year, but now they have to pay 7 percent of that return to the bank, so the return won't be as strong. After subtracting that 7 percent, they will earn 12 percent on DrugMeUp. This means they will earn $1.2 million each year on DrugMeUp, so long as they maintain the loan.

Muffett and Bunger decide to do it! They're smart investors and they know that $3.2 million per year is better than $2 million per year. The overall return on their portfolio of new acquisitions comes out at 16 per-cent — an outstanding ROI — and they go for a steak at their favourite restaurant to celebrate. The only other person by their side is their banker, because they know that without her they wouldn't have had access to an additional $10 million of debt capital and would have lost out on a return of $1.2 million per year.

After dinner they don't light cigars with burning $100 bills to celebrate. Instead, they bury their heads in financial reports because they're going to wake up the next morning and look for more deals like DrugMeUp and JustInCase.

Of course, this is a simplified example. There is much more to analyze than what was mentioned here (like tax, for example), and putting together big debt deals like this (actually, this is rather small in the world of finance) often takes months and even years. But the point remains the same. Smart financial people look at the potential returns on their investment, whether that investment is made with equity capital or debt capital.

The reality for every major corporation and individual is that cash is always in short supply. If businesses only relied on the cash they earned to fund further investments, they would grow their bottom line at a much slower rate. Access to debt capital is a huge momentum-building factor across all sectors of business. I firmly believe that this is an even more important point for individuals seeking a stable and secure retirement than it is for major companies and investment firms. At least the big boys and girls have massive earning potential to fund their growth, but most of us are limited to how much we can earn in a lifetime, unless we happen to be blessed with one of the rare C-level executive positions available in our society.

Given this limitation, we must be very purposeful in our use of debt. Squandering debt capital on fancy toys is a grave sin when we could be using it as a productive asset to deploy in our limited financial arsenal.

Nearly as bad as wasting perfectly good debt capital on a toy is not using debt at all. The opportunity cost of letting equity sit dormant is nearly as damaging to our personal financial position as squandering it is. Because by leaving perfectly good debt equity to rot in prison, we're not taking advantage of the time value of money, which is the topic of our next section.

THE TIME VALUE OF MONEY

What do we mean when we speak about the time value of money? It sounds fancy, but it's actually a very simple concept. It means that money available today is always worth more than the same amount of money at a later date.[17] This is due to compound interest.

Money grows over time, so money from an earlier time is actually worth more than that same amount from a later time. Of course, the individual holding the money must be disciplined enough to actually invest it in order to benefit from the time value of money, but money tends to grow if it is invested wisely. So, if we can, we want to have it invested now rather than later. Failing to have money invested now results in an opportunity cost.

If you have $100,000 now, it is worth $100,000. But in ten years (assuming 7 percent interest), the same $100,000 will be worth $196,715. That's *without* adding any additional outside money. This is simply the power of compounding interest.

The time value of money is why, if you ever win the $80 million Powerball Lotto, you're better off taking a lump sum payment than payouts over a series of years. You could produce a fantastic amount of wealth by investing $80 million today.

The time value of money is why investing works. Investors know that, all things being equal, they are better off getting their money — whether debt or equity — into the market sooner rather than later. But to drive it home, let's look at one of the saddest financial stories I have ever heard. It relates to the time value of money, although most people wouldn't think of it that way. (I'm a bit of a financial geek, in case you haven't noticed.)

I met a man in the real estate investment community who told me about his experience with investing and the financial bind he'd been put in through the combination of life circumstance and an early financial mistake. Like most young people, this man (let's call him Nick) didn't have great financial sense in his early adult years, when he first started earning money. Nick didn't think much beyond each paycheque until he was forty years old. This meant that he didn't have any savings or investments to speak of. He did have a bunch of toys, though, that he'd bought with the equity in his home.

I met Nick when he was fifty years old, and by that time he'd been saving and investing for ten years (he started when he was forty). When they started, Nick and his wife, whom I'll call Marjorie, knew they were behind on investing, so they went to a financial planner to get some help developing a plan that would get them caught up to the best of their ability by the time Nick was sixty-five, when he hoped to retire.

On the positive side, Nick and Marjorie were in a pretty good debt position, having paid off all of his bad consumer debt and having reduced their mortgage quite a bit. Adding to the positivity, Nick earned a strong yearly income as a sales rep. He was a top-notch sales guy and had a degree of control over his yearly income, earning more than $100,000 per year. Marjorie runs a small home-based massage business that brings in a little bit of extra cash.

Nick and Marjorie would have to be aggressive with their savings, but given all the other circumstances, their financial planner helped them put together a plan with which they would save a large portion of their combined income, about $20,000 per year. This would amount to nearly 20 percent of their pre-tax earnings (give or take, depending on his yearly sales numbers and her home-based business earnings). With this level of savings and an estimated return of 6 percent, Nick and Marjorie calculated that they would be able to retire at sixty-five with $1,163,127.65 plus the value of their home, which was $520,000. Of course, the value of the home wasn't much good to them in retirement because they had no intention of selling and neither they nor their financial planner knew how to use debt capital to invest.

Sadly, this is all too common. In this circumstance, the smart use of debt capital for investing could have saved Nick many problems.

When they first made their plan, though, Nick and Marjorie believed that the money, more than $1 million, would be plenty on which to retire. Their home would be free and clear by that time and they didn't expect to have any major expenses upon retirement. They liked to travel but were by no means excessive travellers who needed to spend months at a time abroad. A few weeks at the lake each summer and a warm vacation in the winter were the extent of their travel plans. They also wanted to leave some money for their family. They had two kids who were four and six when they first started investing at age forty.

But when I met him, Nick's plan had been shattered. His savings were nowhere near the level he knew they needed to be. I met him ten years after he and Marjorie had set in motion their aggressive plan to save $20,000 per year. By that time his investment account should have had $279,432.85 in it (compounding at 6 percent), but instead he had less than $40,000.

At age fifty, Nick was beginning his real estate investing career because he knew that he would have to grow his money faster than originally planned. I was happy to have met him at a real estate investing event where he was educating himself. I knew that soon after beginning his journey of real estate investing he'd begin to make quick progress, but we both knew that his dream of retiring at sixty-five was unlikely to happen, although with a little luck it might still.

At the event, Nick learned about the power of borrowing to invest, so he decided to leverage the dormant equity in his home to fund his first investment property. I asked Nick what had happened to his financial plan. This is where it gets sad. He told me how he and his wife had started saving money aggressively right away. Things were going as planned, but then his life met with tragedy.

Within the course of six months, his life changed forever. First, Nick was made redundant at his job. He received a small severance package, but it amounted to only about six months' worth of salary. He would need every bit of that money to hold him over until he could get himself a new job. The first thing to take a hit was his savings strategy.

Then real tragedy struck: Marjorie was diagnosed with a rare form of cancer that rendered her unable to work. Compounding the problem, there was no proven treatment, but there were experimental treatments being offered in Germany that they were willing to try. Of course, these were very costly, and now you know why Nick's savings were so meager ten years after he'd put his plan into motion. Sadly, Marjorie passed away a couple of years after her diagnosis. But not before she and Nick had spent everything they had trying to save her life.

What does this have to do with the time value of money? Tragedy can strike anyone. Obviously health is primary over wealth, and Nick would have spent all that money on treatments again in a heartbeat. There was nothing anyone could have done about the cancer, but with a little more luck and advance planning, Nick and Marjorie would have started their investment savings much earlier. The principle of the time value of money states that having put aside even a smaller amount of money earlier would have put them in a more beneficial financial position by the time the tragedy struck. Nick still would have lost his job. Marjorie still would have gotten cancer. They still would have spent the same amount of money on her treatments. But since they would have had a lot more money in their coffers, the blow wouldn't have been as devastating.

Here's the thing: Nick is a tough guy. Many circumstances conspired against him. He didn't have any financial education early in his life. He had been a typical young man, more caught up in spending his money than investing it. Then the real tragedies struck. But even at age fifty, I knew he would come out okay. He'd got another job soon after losing his other job, and he started saving again after Marjorie passed away.

But most importantly, he was learning the right things, even if it was a bit late in life. There is still plenty to be positive about at age fifty if you start putting dormant equity to work in the real estate market and then purchase cash-flow-positive properties.

Nick will very likely be working past age sixty-five, when he wanted to retire, but he didn't seem so concerned about that. He knew he was building a strong financial future and that his kids would eventually inherit his properties. He planned on giving them more than just the properties, though. His plan was to educate them on the principles of wealth creation he hadn't learned until much later in life. His actions would ensure that, even though he hadn't profited from the time value of money as much in his life as he could have, his kids and their kids would.

THE HIGHEST AND BEST USE OF CAPITAL

Here's how I think of my money — as soldiers — I send them out to war everyday. I want them to take prisoners and come home so there's more of them.

— KEVIN O'LEARY

Remember the investors Muffett and Bunger? They found the highest and best use of capital. They never let money just sit around doing nothing. Lazy money is kicked out of its home and sent out into the world to work or, as Kevin O'Leary says, to war.

The principle of finding the highest and best use of capital is simple to understand. Of course, in the real world we sometimes don't know what the exact highest and best use will be. We might think our mutual fund investments will be a higher and better use than real estate, for example, only to find out later that they aren't.

We can't know for sure, but what we can know is that capital is doing nothing for us if it's not out in the world working. This rule applies to both debt and equity capital. Cash, of course, must be put to work, but if we have a way to access debt capital and yet still fail to put it to work, it means we're letting our money be lazy.

Real estate — especially cash flow properties (as opposed to real estate funds) — might be the highest and best use of money because of our ability to leverage it so dramatically. Only in real estate are we able to take already leveraged money and turn it into five times more money.

Let's look at an example to explain what I mean: Imagine you have $60,000 worth of dormant equity. You come talk to me and learn that you can access that $60,000 to invest in cash-flowing real estate. Then you go find a property worth $300,000 and buy it. The initial $60,000 of available dormant equity is for the down payment, and then we secure you a mortgage for the other $240,000 to purchase the property. Now you own $300,000 worth of assets, rather than $60,000. But if you were to take the same $60,000 and invest it in non–real estate assets, you would be purchasing only $60,000 worth of assets. In the real estate example, if the market appreciates by 3 percent, you'll actually be earning a 15 percent return on the initial $60,000 invested.

$300,000 × 3 percent = $9,000
$9,000 ÷ $60,000 = 15 percent

Articles about personal finance often trumpet the better long-term returns attained in the stock market than in the real estate market. One such article stated that real estate earned 5.5 percent annually over a thirty-year period, while the benchmark TSX earned 8.5 percent.[18]

I don't dispute the numbers, but articles of this type usually leave out the fact that real estate allows you to invest five times more money. So rather than earning 5.5 percent over thirty years, the smart real estate investor would have earned 27.5 percent (5.5 × 5). Suddenly real estate looks pretty good.

Another problem with articles of this kind is that they make it seem like investors have to make a choice between the stock market and real estate. There isn't a financial planner alive worth his or her name that would recommend being fully invested in a single asset class. Smart investors, seeking wise advice from a financial planner, will always be invested across a variety of asset classes, including both real estate and stocks. Being invested exclusively in real estate without an RRSP and other assets in stock or other non–real estate investments is not wise. Equally unwise is being all in stocks but not having any real estate other than your principal residence.

One of the great things about a good financial planner is that they will recommend investing in real estate to their clients, even though it falls outside the realm of traditional investments. Their concern is the highest and best use of capital, and this will always include some portion of real estate. But, depending on market conditions, the percentage of the portfolio made up of real estate will fluctuate. Great financial planners also know that long-term diversification is the best way to grow and sustain wealth.

Your concern should also be the highest and best use of capital. To practice this, use whatever capital is available to you, whether debt capital or equity capital. Also, have at least some portion of your capital invested in cash-flowing real estate, where you will be able to leverage up to five times more money than would otherwise be possible.

UNDERSTANDING INTEREST DEDUCTIBILITY

Paying tax is unavoidable, but most Canadians don't realize that they can dramatically reduce their tax bill while at the same time building a retirement investment portfolio.

Our American cousins are gifted with a powerful tool for wealth creation the moment they purchase a home. In the United States, mortgage interest is tax deductible (even on your personal-use home). The result is that, year after year, millions of Americans receive a tax refund courtesy of Uncle Sam.

Canadian tax law doesn't allow for this. When we borrow money to purchase a principal residence, we pay interest on that money. Over the lifetime of the mortgage, the interest paid dramatically inflates the total amount paid back in addition to the principal of the loan. The interest kills us.

Imagine if we could deduct a large portion of that expense off our taxes every year. What kind of difference would it make over the lifetime of your mortgage? The answer is a lot. Imagine you have a $400,000 mortgage on your home residence at 3 percent. Even in the low-interest-rate environment of today, you'd still pay $169,053.58 in interest over the twenty-five year life of the loan.

Thinking in terms of the time value of money and the highest and best use of capital, that's a simply enormous amount of money gone, never to return to you. But what can you do, right? It's the price of owning a home.

Sort of. If you understand interest deductibility, you will do a few things differently, and in a roundabout way you will get some of the lost interest payments back in the form of a tax deduction.

As you know, borrowing to invest in real estate or other asset classes is one of the most important steps you can take to ensure you have a stable and secure retirement. In a moment, we'll discuss the proper steps for maximizing interest deductibility, but first let's make sure we have a rudimentary understanding of interest deductibility.

But before launching into that, here would be a good place for another reminder to always seek professional advice from a licensed and proven tax accountant. Few things in the realm of personal finance more resemble a Pandora's Box than the world of taxes. Nothing you read in this book should be considered tax advice. But it's important to discuss basic deductibility, since it's a key concept of borrowing to invest.

It comes down to this: Interest paid on money borrowed to invest can be deducted off your tax bill. Interest paid on money borrowed for other reasons cannot. The Income Tax Act allows you to deduct any interest expenses if the borrowed money is invested "to produce income."[19] Again, consult with your accountant for professional advice. The point remains, though, that we have found a way to minimize tax expense. All we have to do is borrow money for the purpose of investing.

This can help you (immediately) on your personal residence. You'll never be able to deduct interest on the portion of the mortgage that is used to purchase your principal residence, but you can borrow additional funds against your home for the purpose of investing, thereby creating a tax-deductible interest expense.

Additionally, please be aware that the interest paid on money borrowed for personal reasons isn't tax deductible. This includes those luxurious liabilities. Not only are expensive toys a terrible "investment," but they're also not beneficial toward an effective tax strategy. The only way to create a tax advantage through borrowing is to borrow for the purpose of investment. It's the next best thing to having what our American neighbours have.

So, what should you do now that you know about interest deductibility on funds borrowed for the purpose of investing? First, always be leveraged when it fits your financial and psychological profile. Leverage your personal residence and put that money to work in the marketplace. Second, deduct the allowable interest expense from your taxes. Hire a great accountant who can help you with this. Third, don't borrow money for toys. If you need to buy fun luxuries, please wait until you have the financial means to do so with cash. Fourth, always consider the after-tax cost of borrowing and the after-tax rate of return when analyzing investment debts and returns. This final step is the topic of our next section and a step that financial wizards always take.

AFTER-TAX COST OF BORROWING AND RATE OF RETURN

Imagine you're buying winter tires for your car — as most Canadians have done — and you have a $100 rebate. The original price of the tires is $650, but with the rebate you'll pay only $550.

At the same time there is another set of tires with a cheaper sticker price, only $600, but you don't have a rebate for this second set of tires. To get the rebate on the first set of tires, you have to fill in a form and send it away. The money will come in the mail in a couple of weeks.

Which is a better deal?

Even if the $650 set of tires was merely equal in quality to the $600 set of tires, you would pay less to purchase it. I imagine you would take the rebate into account when calculating your purchase decision. Yes, you would have to pay $50 more at the shop when they put your tires on, but in a matter of a couple of weeks you would get more back. It's a straightforward example, and I hope everyone would do the right thing and purchase the tires with the rebate. This is essentially what financial experts do when it comes to investments. When analyzing, they take into account the after-tax numbers.

Consumers must act the same way in order to create wealth to fund their retirement. Let's assume John and Jane took out $200,000 of dormant equity at 3 percent on a five-year fixed mortgage — a very reasonable assumption in today's market. This means that their stellar interest rate is locked in for five years, which creates cost stability. But instead of going on a long vacation, John and Jane decide to follow the example of the top financial minds. They're now using debt capital to invest, and they want to put it to its highest and best use.

John and Jane are in the top tax bracket. For simplicity's sake, let's say they're giving up 45 percent on their federal and provincial tax. John and Jane have read this book, so they know the power of borrowing to invest, and they also know that the interest on their borrowed-for-investment funds is tax deductible. The tax deduction effectively means that, instead of paying 3 percent interest on their borrowed funds, they will be paying 1.65 percent interest (3 percent × [1 − 0.45]), adjusting for the tax rate and reflecting the after-tax cost of 55 percent. As with the rebate on the tires, John and Jane would have to fill out a few forms in order to get the tax deduction.

It gets a bit more complicated, of course. Because John and Jane are go-getters, they've managed to deploy the entire $200,000 into real estate purchases by using it as a down payment. This means they've turned their $200,000 into $1 million worth of real estate assets, all earning cash flow. The new mortgages they took out to cover the remaining 80 percent also have 3 percent interest rates.

John and Jane are smart. They bought great properties in great neighbourhoods, did detailed analyses of each one, and brought on a great team to help them. Because they bought well, every expense, including the interest on the initial money (formerly dormant equity) *and* the interest on the remaining $800,000 is being paid by the rental income of the properties. They are paying 3 percent interest on $1 million worth of debt. That's $30,000 per year. (This figure is rough and will change as the principal goes down.)

Meanwhile, John and Jane are thinking ahead to next year's tax time. They want to pay as little as they can on their tax bill, and they know that they're entitled to deduct 45 percent of the cost of the interest. Using round numbers, this means they'll end up paying only 1.6 percent interest, rather than 3 percent. Doing the calculation, 1.6 percent of $1 million is $16,000. Now they're paying (correction — their tenants are paying) only $16,000 for the deployment of $1 million worth of investment funds. That's incredibly cheap money.

But John and Jane think and act like financial wizards, so they're not done calculating. At the end of the first year, they get an appraisal on their new portfolio and find out it has appreciated 5 percent. They're very happy. "Did we just make an additional $50,000 on top of our salaries?" they ask. Then they remember that they only care about the after-tax rate of return, just as they only care about the after-tax cost of borrowing. Damn. Now they will have to give the government back 45 percent of their new-found $50,000. Or will they?

John and Jane have a great team, including a wise tax accountant (a gold medalist referred by me) who explains to them the beauty of capital gains, which aren't taxed like regular income. First off, they won't have to pay any capital gains tax on their properties until they sell, but they're smart, so they know that all this appreciation will eventually lead to paying tax on their capital gains.

But their tax accountant gives them some more good news. They will be taxed on only half of their capital gains. So, rather than being taxed 45 percent on $50,000, they will be taxed 45 percent on $25,000, for a total tax expense of $11,250. It still stings, but John and Jane would rather pay $11,250 than the $22,500 they would have been forced to pay if they had earned an extra $50,000 on their salaries.

Then again, there was never any risk that they would make an extra $50,000 on their salaries, at least not this year. Instead, they earned $38,500 on their $1 million invested, for an after-tax return of 3.85 percent on the debt capital invested. John and Jane are happy because they know that they never would have found $1 million to invest without the use of debt capital.

I urge you to be like John and Jane.

STAY INVESTED

Our favourite holding period is forever.

— WARREN BUFFETT

Let's fast-forward four years in John and Jane's story. They've had three good years in a row now, and each year the market appreciated between 3 and 5 percent, which is consistent with the averaged-out long-term historical trend for real estate. But their first three profitable years of real estate investing were at the end of a rather long run-up in the market. John and Jane knew this day would come. On year four, it was time for a correction in the marketplace.

Before getting into real estate, John and Jane consulted with a knowledgeable mortgage professional, a financial planner, a real estate agent, and other important team members. Every one of their team members told them the same story, which essentially went like this: "Whenever an asset class over-performs, you can expect there to be a market correction."

It was difficult. The real estate assets John and Jane bought for $1 million four years ago were at one point valued as high as $1,150,000. But values went down 7 percent during the correction on the fourth year, which meant the total value of their portfolio dropped all the way down to $1,069,500.

Of course it's frustrating, but John and Jane had been forewarned. Luckily they stayed in touch with their team, since they were considering new purchases in the near future. The team continued to remind them that this day would come, that it was natural, and that the correct course of action was to stay invested. It's not until the second appreciation run during ownership when the true gains are often made.

John and Jane decided to stick it out. They will keep their properties, wait out this down spell in the market, and continue to hold through the next years, when they expect the market to continue its historical trend toward growth. Furthermore, they are looking at ways of purchasing more property right now, during this market lull.

This is where John and Jane are different than most retail investors, who often tuck tail and run at the most inopportune time. This is where human intuition fails us. As investors, we must train ourselves out of the human tendency to flee what appears to be a dangerous situation. John and Jane are rational, slow, deliberate thinkers.

Are you currently, or can you train yourself to think that way?

There's a simple way to help you stay invested through market lulls. Ask yourself this simple yet critical question: is this a real loss, or only a loss on paper? Knowing what we know about all markets, including real estate, we can say with reasonable certainty that the markets will rebound and soon John and Jane's real estate holdings will appreciate again.

Great investors know that market carnage is a buy signal and that market growth is a sell signal, but too many retail investors get it backwards. They buy real estate, and the market drops, so they sell their real estate. Then they jump into stocks because they've heard they're doing well. Instead of understanding that stocks "doing well" is a sell signal, they jump in as buyers. When the stock market correction comes, they jump out, saying, "The stock market is crooked."

We'll talk a bit about risk mitigation in the next section. For now I'd just like to mention that one of the best risk mitigating strategies is to know your investment horizon. Don't jump into any investment without understanding that you might have to hold paper losses through a market lull.

ALWAYS INVEST, DON'T SPECULATE

John and Jane spent time educating themselves. As I counselled in the first section of this book, they didn't over-educate themselves, but they did read several books, join a real estate investment club, and learn from other investors and team members. One of the first things they learned was the benefit of investing rather than speculating. What's the difference? Speculation is when you buy an asset with only the hope that it will go up in value.[20] It's essentially a calculated risk, but the key point is that the only way to make money on a speculation is if the asset goes up in value. Speculation also has a connotation of high turnover to it. You're making the money on the trade.

Speculation sounds like a lot of fun, doesn't it? It's probably not going to be a lot of fun if you're playing with money you need to build a retirement with. John and Jane learned about speculation from the real estate group they joined. They thought maybe one day, once their retirement was completely funded, they might like to speculate with a small percentage of their money, but they certainly weren't going to be speculating any time soon. First, they needed to build the retirement they wanted. Through their education, they knew they would have to use the timeless principles employed by top financial minds — those discussed in this chapter.

One of these timeless principles is the need to invest rather than speculate. Investing differs from speculation in that you can earn income in many ways, even if the value of the asset remains stagnant or goes down. Investing has a long-term connotation to it. You don't have to make money by trading anything. Instead you hold, and the asset is productive while you own it.[21]

John and Jane knew this, which is why they committed to staying in the market rather than pulling out their money. Even investing is risky, which is why smart investors take steps to diversify and mitigate risk.

For diversification, you will need to see a world-class financial planner. For further proper risk mitigation, you will want to consult with a team of qualified professionals, such as accountants, real estate agents, mortgage professionals with a financial planning education (like me), property inspectors, and many more. We will discuss the major risk mitigation strategies.

Investing well comes down to this: Stay away from get-rich-quick schemes and any form of speculating. Stay with time-honoured, diversified, risk-averse investment strategies. By sticking to a solid plan, like the real estate retirement plan, almost anyone can overcome the tendency to make poor financial decisions and become true investors.

ARE YOU USING CAPITAL WELL?

Ask yourself the following questions to self-assess whether you're treating capital, wealth creation, and investing like the financial wizards of the world would:

- Do you know that debt is a type of capital?
- Do you use debt to purchase productive assets?
- Do you believe that equity capital is the only type of money available for investing?
- Do you understand the time value of money?
- Do you take advantage of the time value of money?
- Do you realize that debt capital, wisely deployed, also helps you take advantage of the time value of money?
- Do you seek to put both debt capital and equity capital to work to their highest and best use?
- Do you understand and calculate the real (after-tax) cost of borrowing and rates of return?
- Do you understand your own psychology and the mentality of retail investors?
- Have you educated yourself to understand that market growth is a sell signal and market stagnation is a buy signal?
- Do you understand that hot markets always correct eventually?
- Do you know the difference between speculation and investing?
- Are you getting (or do you already have) the education to invest long-term in the real estate market?
- Do you have a financial planner to help you create a balanced portfolio that performs well?

LEARNING TO THINK AND ACT LIKE THE MASTERS OF MONEY

In this chapter we discussed the mindset, thinking, and, most importantly, actions of the top financial experts. We've learned that there are very real differences between such experts and the average person seeking a stable and secure retirement.

Chances are, you likely already understood much of what we discussed in this chapter, but I bet there have been many times when you didn't act in accordance with these principles. I'm not trying to be some kind of oracle, but I can bet you've broken these principles because everyone has. It's just human nature. We are deeply flawed in the way we act because we don't always (or even often) consult our rational, slow-thinking minds. Instead we feel fear or greed and act on impulse, like a pack of wolves on the hunt or a herd of caribou running from danger.

The best thing you can do to bring these principles into your awareness is to continue studying, practising, educating, speaking to experts, and surrounding yourself with like-minded individuals who are on the same path. These principles aren't difficult to understand, but executing them will require you to overcome the all-too-human emotions of fear and greed. This is difficult when your money is on the line.

CHAPTER 6
Borrowing to Invest in Real Estate

Ninety percent of all millionaires become so through owning real estate.
— Andrew Carnegie

THE TRUTH BEHIND REAL ESTATE MILLIONAIRES

It's commonly stated that real estate creates more millionaires than any other investment class. However, what's less often mentioned is that this is possible because of the power of borrowing to invest and the conservative use of leverage.

While using leverage is, and has been, available for other types of investment, these are less well-known, and the average person typically hasn't understood the mechanism for leveraged investing in stocks, for example. To be clear, borrowing to invest in other asset classes is possible. But borrowing to invest in real estate has certain benefits that other asset classes don't provide, especially for the retirement-focused investor.

Borrowing to invest in real estate is not only simple, but it is, in fact, the expected course of action. Without leverage, most real estate purchasers would only be dreamers. Most people could never afford to buy even a modest real estate property with only equity capital (broadly defined as the saved down payment). We almost always must create debt to purchase real estate, and thus we put more capital to work in the market than would otherwise be possible.

In this chapter, we'll discuss the ins and outs of borrowing money to invest in real estate, especially as it pertains to creating a stable and secure retirement. We'll talk about freeing up dormant home equity for investing, which lets us put far more capital in the market. We'll discuss how borrowing money for real estate investments is the best solution available for producing a monthly coupon, which in many ways can mimic a pension fund. We'll talk about how simple it is to borrow money for the purpose of investing in real estate and about the compounding growth of a portfolio, as each subsequent property purchased becomes a new potential source of investment capital and as each property's value rises over time and new equity goes dormant. In addition, we'll discuss how to mitigate risk when borrowing to invest and the conditions under which you should or shouldn't consider this potentially life-altering course of action.

But first we'll take a look at the initial considerations that every investor must keep in mind before participating in any borrow-to-invest strategy. These points form a broad guideline to follow, but, as always, develop a detailed plan with your financial planner before embarking on such a financial strategy, especially one as important (and leveraged) as a borrow-to-invest strategy.

BORROW-TO-INVEST PRECAUTIONARY PLANNING

Yes, I'm a believer in borrowing to invest, but I don't want you to get the false impression that my optimism for this strategy amounts to a blind acceptance of it. It's important to follow solid investment guidelines — in fact, it's a deal-breaker if you don't. If you don't fit the financial and psychological profile and have the right team to make sure you do it right, then please don't execute this strategy.

When engaging in the use of home equity to borrow to invest, you must take extra precautions to ensure you're never put at major risk. We want to ensure that you are never put in a mortgage crisis situation as a result of not taking sound precautions. These precautions aren't elaborate, yet they form a solid foundation upon which to make borrow-to-invest decisions.

Get Objective Advice

Your financial planner may be biased because he or she does not stand to make additional commissions if you leverage to buy real estate. There are many excellent fee-based financial planners in the world, and this should be a key component of your financial planner selection process. But the fact remains that most financial planners make their income from commissions. This is not good, because there is no scenario in which the goals of a commission-based financial planner match perfectly with the goals of a client.

But even non-fee-based financial planners stand to benefit by having more assets under management. The same can be said about financial planning–focused mortgage professionals like myself. My office also stands to benefit when you increase your loan size or take out a new mortgage. A great financial advisor will be transparent about potential conflicts of interest. Personally, I always want my investment manager's fees to grow when my portfolio grows and to decline when my portfolio declines.

To get a more even-handed opinion, talk to an accountant before borrowing any significant sum. The tax benefits of this strategy are a key component of what makes it profitable for people. Before you act on advice, be sure the person is qualified to give it — this is the bottom line.

Build In a Margin of Safety

To determine how large an investment loan you should consider, calculate the size of loan you can comfortably afford to finance. Then reduce this amount by any potential downturn you may face. A "downturn" could mean a loss of income or an increase in expenses. I advise all clients to make sure they have a margin of safety for both their cash-flow requirements and their unplanned expenses. Doing this will mean that a forced liquidation (sale) isn't also a cash-flow crunch at the same time. It very rarely makes sense to borrow the maximum amount a lender thinks you can handle, unless you have a unique set of circumstances, such as considerable liquid investments to help you weather market turmoil. Lenders' goals are not necessarily aligned with your own. The name of the game here is conservative leverage, which isn't to be confused with irresponsible leverage.

Building in a margin of safety means that you will be able to afford any unforeseen income drops or interest rate risks you may face. In addition, always maintain an emergency cash reserve, regardless of loan selection.

Know How the Numbers Work

The arithmetic of leveraging is a function of interest rates, your tax rate, your returns, and the type of returns (capital gains, dividends, or interest generally). When these change, re-evaluate your strategy and the real rate of return after tax. It is easy to lose some of the interest deductibility on an investment loan if you sell a portion of the leveraged investments or if the investments are certain to return less than the loan interest rate, as would be the case with a bond or low-yield real estate investment. You must understand the basic tax rules, as well as the tax efficiency of your investments, and keep on top of interest rates. Stay up to date yourself and seek the best advice available from your team.

Commit to the Long Term, but Keep Your Options Open

A leveraging strategy should only be used if you are committed to it for the long term. I can't stress enough how critical this is. I personally recommend that no borrowing-to-invest strategy for stocks or real estate have shorter than a ten-year investment horizon, and this strategy should never be considered for a hold cycle of less than five years. But you will feel more comfortable if you build in an escape hatch by purchasing only quality investments that can be easily sold without serious penalty. If you choose to do this, then understand there is a correlation between risk and return. Not only do less risky investments return less, but they also tend to generate less in capital gains, which is the ideal return for the simple fact that it gets the most preferential tax treatment.

Real estate is relatively non-liquid, and you will be penalized in the form of fees and capital gains tax. However, so long as your safety margin is maintained, you should be able to sell your real estate property in a relatively short period of time if crisis should demand it. Ensuring you have cash on hand to tide you over between the crisis and the asset sale is a wise move.

But these are all worst-case scenarios: important to consider and plan for, but worst-case scenarios nonetheless. Barring the unexpected, I urge you to always go into a borrow-to-invest strategy with the long term in mind.

Following these simple steps will take you a long way on your decision to borrow to invest, but now let's turn to some of the benefits of borrowing to invest in real estate specifically.

THE SECURITY OF BORROWING TO INVEST IN REAL ESTATE

One of the most common concerns for investors is security. Putting aside the complete lack of security that many people use their leveraged funds for (buying liabilities), any leveraged money adds an element of insecurity to our financial life.

In a worst-case scenario, it's never a good feeling when we lose our own money. But what can be even worse is when we lose the bank's money, because that has long-term reputational and financial consequences for you as a consumer and, potentially, for life.

Warren Buffett (who, as you might have guessed by now, I am a big fan of) says this well: "Rule number one: Never lose money. Rule number two: Never forget rule number one."

Wise investors, rightfully, seek a high level of security when borrowing to invest. We live in a nation and time in which not borrowing to invest might be the riskiest thing we do. Failing to do so may very well result in us having to reduce our quality of life during retirement. But the last thing anyone wants to do is potentially sabotage that retirement plan by losing the borrowed money. Consider return *of* capital, not just return *on* capital.

Here's the thing: borrowing to invest in stable, positive-cash-flowing real estate or even high-quality blue-chip dividend-paying stocks, when well executed, is the lowest risk measure you can take to dramatically improve your retirement standard of living and prospects. Borrowing to invest in real estate has the key benefit that you have a directly agreed-upon offsetting payment that addresses your debt. In other words: rent.

Every debt must be serviced. There are balloon payment loans and the like, but in order to access the preferred stable, low-interest-rate bank money, you'll have to service the loan with a payment every month. If you have to pay interest using another source of your own money, the debt doesn't make sense. The investment must cover its own payments.

As far as borrowing to invest in something with a stable coupon repayment, there is nothing that compares to real estate in terms of coupon stability. You could try your luck with Government of Canada bonds, but that wouldn't produce enough cash flow. At any rate, you would never be able to service your debt on the micro-returns provided in today's bond and money market environment. As a matter of fact, the low returns from Canada Savings Bonds will actually leave you poorer by year end, once you take inflation into consideration.

While you can purchase dividend-producing stocks and other investments, their returns are nowhere near as carved-in-stone as real estate's are. When you execute real estate well, on the other hand, you gain a high degree of certainty and stability of cash flows. The third section of this book will provide you with a primer on how to properly execute on real estate. But the points to remember are these: a) it's not that difficult to do; and b) you have a high degree of control over a private real estate investment, whereas you have no control over a stock investment.

In real estate, the tenants service (and indeed pay down) your debt for you. I don't know many things for certain, but here's one that I can stand behind: there will always be a need for people to have a place to live. You can't that say with as much certainty about many companies, if any. They may pay a strong dividend when you buy, but you can't guarantee the same dividend over the long term.

As to the second point, you have no control over the company once you've invested in it. But, by proactively managing your real estate investment, you can stand out from the crowd and make your property more appealing than that of the competition, which increases the value of your security as your vacancy rate goes down. But even if you're a mediocre landlord in a strong market, vacancy rates are incredibly low in all the stable rental markets of Canada.

This is the basic level of security that borrowing to invest in real estate provides. Other asset classes can't compete in this way. It's a major reason why I believe a significant chunk of your borrowed investment funds should be plugged into real estate.

THE SIMPLICITY OF BORROWING TO INVEST IN REAL ESTATE

I could give you hundreds of examples about how simple it is to borrow to invest in real estate, but I'll choose just one.

A client came into our office recently wanting to invest in her first rental property. Let's call her Jen. She had been working hard and diligently saving for the past ten years and was now ready to start investing. Luckily (and wisely) for Jen, she is still young enough to benefit greatly from the time value of money. Jen's plan was to use the cash she'd saved to fund the down payment on her first rental property — a wise plan. Jen wanted to buy a rental property with high cash flow for under $400,000 in one of the towns surrounding Toronto. This was another wise decision, especially because of the monthly cash flow it would create.

Our team was thrilled to help Jen. She's smart and diligent, and she was about to make some incredibly good financial decisions. However, we knew that with a few tweaks she could do even better. Jen had saved up $80,000 and was ready to use that money to purchase her new investment property. But we wanted her to achieve the best results possible, so we introduced her to the idea of borrowing to invest.

"But aren't I already doing that? That's why I'm here, after all, taking out a mortgage to buy a property," she said.

True. This is most folks' reaction the first time they hear about the concept. "But you could also borrow the down payment. Then you wouldn't have to use the cash you've saved as a down payment funds. You can either keep that as an emergency fund or keep some and invest the rest in another asset class," I said.

Of course, she was a bit skeptical. Everyone should be skeptical and truly think through the consequences of every major financial decision they make. But Jen is smart, and she was ready to hear me out. So she listened patiently as I explained the merits of turning her dormant home equity to an investment in real estate.

Jen had owned her home for the past ten years. That alone told me that her home had appreciated. The entire Toronto real estate market had been strong over that entire time, but the same could be said for pretty much any stable Canadian market over a long-term cycle.

I asked her if she had refinanced her home in the past ten years. She informed me that she hadn't. At the end of her initial five-year term, she had gone back to the bank and renewed the mortgage. As of that moment, her second five-year term was soon coming to an end.

Jen knew that real estate had done well since she'd purchased her home, but she didn't know exactly how well. We took all the information we needed from Jen that day, and she agreed to think about the idea of getting two mortgages instead of one. The first, if she chose, would be a mortgage on her principal residence, with which she would remove a large amount of dormant equity to fund the down payment on her first (and perhaps second and third) rental property. For tax purposes, the incremental money taken out of her principal residence would have to be kept separate from her non–tax-deductible debt. The other mortgage would be to finance the remaining 80 percent of the purchase price of her first rental property.

She came back to our office a few days later and said she wanted to go for it — in her case, a wise financial decision. We got started with the mortgage application and all the other steps required. To mortgage her principal residence, we needed to get an appraisal on the home. Jen was a little bit surprised to find out how much her home was actually worth in today's market.

She'd bought it back in 2006 for $350,000. When we got it appraised in 2016, it was worth $650,000. This meant that, even after leaving 20 percent of the equity untouched, she would have access to $200,000. Now, instead of just investing the initial $80,000 of cash she had saved, Jen was contemplating the prospect of investing $280,000 from a combination of equity capital and debt capital.

A week later we had the approval. Three weeks later she had an accepted offer on her first rental property. Five weeks later she owned her first rental property, already tenanted and cash flowing. Nine weeks later she made her first mortgage payments on her two new loans. The rental income covered all of the expenses on the property, including the portion of her principal residence mortgage that went to purchasing her new rental property.

Because of the flexibility of today's mortgage products, Jen still has a big chunk of equity available. She's not paying any interest on that portion, but I don't think it will remain dormant for long. When she decides to purchase another property, she will be able to access the remaining dormant equity almost instantaneously. She is only buying property that has positive cash flow now and that could sustain a rise of up to 3 percent in the level of interest rates. This is a mechanism I consider to be a prudent consideration for extra protection. We *always* stress-test properties like this before buying. Clients must have sufficient cash flow to survive interest rate fluctuations and enough liquid finances to pay for unexpected expenses.

All of this was incredibly easy. The mere fact that Jen had purchased a home ten years ago was enough to ensure she had access to borrowed funds. There are a few other factors at play, of course. Jen had strong debt service numbers, which also helped her. But generally speaking, her situation is extremely common across this country. Many people have dormant equity merely due to the fact that they purchased real estate many years ago. The combination of appreciation and principal repayment has built up considerable equity. There has even been a phrase coined to describe such people: the mass affluent. The term refers to the large group of Canadians whose balance sheets show significant assets, most often locked away, unused, in their homes.

Are you a member of the mass affluent?

Jen was and she didn't even know it. Because of this mass affluent phenomenon and the flexibility of mortgage products today, it was ridiculously simple for Jen to turn herself into a real estate investor, and (here's the important part) she did it without taking a huge risk. Her numbers were extremely safe and we stress-tested them in our model before investing.

In this book, we teach you how to borrow to invest. You probably already knew about the need for a standard mortgage to buy an investment property, but perhaps you didn't know about using debt capital pulled from your own home (or maybe an existing rental property) to fund the down payment for a rental property.

You might also know by now that you could take dormant equity out of your home to invest in stocks, but there is a problem with this strategy — it doesn't typically provide the debt service coverage that rental real estate does.

There are other ways to borrow to invest in other asset classes. You can do a leveraged loan against a stock portfolio as well, but it's not as simple as with real estate. Leveraged loans against marketable real estate are amongst the easiest to qualify for, have the lowest interest rates, and have the most options available. The banks love to lend for real estate. Just look at the leverage levels they allow compared to other types of assets. Eighty percent LTV (loan-to-value) loans are the norm in real estate today. I doubt you will be able to find another asset class in which you can borrow such a high percentage of the total value and *still* get such preferential rates and conditions. If you're buying positive cash-flowing property and maintaining good credit and net worth, it is (comparatively) easy to borrow at cost-effective rates with a (relatively) limited amount of paperwork.

Think about how quick and simple it was for Jen. *Her story isn't unique.* My office is doing deals like that every single day. She's not some wealthy trust fund kid or investing genius — just another (mostly accidental) mass affluent Canadian who decided to take some action.

Lenders like the fact that people like Jen borrow to invest in appreciable assets. They are more lenient in such cases. Even though they often do it, the wiser of the bankers will hesitate if you tell them you want to take equity out of your home to buy a liability.

Be like Jen if you can. Rather than putting only $80,000 of equity capital into the marketplace, put a combined $280,000 worth of debt and equity capital, then leverage that up by purchasing cash-flowing real estate. Couldn't you stand to earn $3,386,354 more over twenty-five years? It's relatively easy to do for mass affluent Canadians, and a team like mine can help you make it a reality in a reasonably short amount of time. The example in the next section will show you how.

PUTTING THE PRINCIPLES TO WORK

What difference would investing $280,000 make over a twenty-five year period? Well, due to a pair of financial principles, it would make an incredible difference. Let's take a look at some projected numbers. Of course, we can only make educated assumptions, but based on history we can make those assumptions with a degree of confidence.

First let's look at the scenario where Jen only invests her $80,000 in savings. Imagine she invests it today and earns 7 percent on her money. After twenty-five years she would have a total value of $434,194. That's not bad. But she can do much better.

What if she invested $280,000 today? Jen wants to be prudent, so let's imagine she invests the $80,000 of unleveraged money (equity capital) in proven blue chip stocks. Again let's assume 7 percent. So she still has her $434,194 on that front. But Jen knows about investing debt capital now, so she's decided to put the $200,000 of dormant equity from her principal residence to work in the market. Here she decides to invest in real estate because she knows that the monthly coupon it provides a safe way to ensure her monthly debt expense would be covered by the investment income.

With the three real estate profit centres (cash flow plus mortgage pay-down plus appreciation), let's assume an extremely conservative 5 percent return. The market average over longer periods is more like 5.5 percent simply on appreciation (ignoring cash flow and mortgage pay-down), but for the sake of this example let's assume a safe 5 percent. Now Jen has earned $677,271 for a total portfolio value of $1,111,465 — a huge improvement. Assuming Jen retires in twenty-five years, she would have an additional $677,271 in her retirement account.

I realize that I sound like a cheesy late-night infomercial salesman for saying this: *but wait, there's more!* One of the incredible things about borrowing to invest in real estate strategy is that it not only puts your own borrowed funds from your principal residence to work, but it also lets you unlock 80 percent more money.

Jen bought one investment property, but she can soon spin the rest of the borrowed money into real estate investment purchases. So, let's imagine she puts the entire $200,000 of equity into real estate. When leveraged up, this means she's purchasing $1 million worth of real estate. Twenty percent of the purchase value would come from the formerly dormant equity in her principal residence. The bank will provide the other $800,000 to purchase the properties in the form of new mortgages. Now instead of investing only $280,000, Jen will invest $1,080,000 in total ($80,000 cash savings plus $200,000 formerly dormant equity plus $800,000 new mortgage financing).

Let's continue with the conservative prediction model of 5 percent. Over twenty-five years this would add an additional $2,709,083. For those of you keeping track at home (and I hope you all are), the total value of Jen's investments would now be $3,820,548. That's a net worth improvement of $3,386,354 ($3,820,548 total value minus $434,194 value if only investing equity capital). Most of her growth in wealth would be capital gains and thus taxed preferentially compared to other types of income. She would only be taxed when selling, but she may never choose to sell.

This is the difference between funding two or three real estate properties (early in the financial cycle) with debt capital versus only investing equity capital. Of course, Jen's plan was to purchase real estate using her savings, so she would have received some of the added benefit I've mentioned. But the example of investing only the equity capital in stocks or mutual funds is what folks commonly do, which is why I provided Jen's example here. Even great savers like Jen would earn just a fraction of the return by investing savings only into standard investments like mutual funds (forget about the erosion of returns due to excessive fees).

But wait, there's more. (It's even cheesier the second time.)

If Jen gets the exact returns we're imagining here, it's really just the beginning of her benefit. She then would have to make a decision. She would have all of those millions on her balance sheet. She may sell and thus take home a huge windfall but also trigger a large capital gains tax, or she may just continue to hold them. If she holds them, she will earn several thousand dollars per month on rental income. This would effectively be her pension in addition to the tiny slice of CPP she might receive. Or she might refinance her properties (in fact, I hope she will refinance several times in the intervening years), buy more real estate, and continue along the same path.

How would you like to have nearly $4 million on your balance sheet, plus thousands in monthly passive income in twenty-five years?

Jen's example shows us the incredible power of borrowing to invest in real estate and holding it over the long term. What I love about her scenario is that it's not far-fetched. Millions of "mass affluent" Canadians can do what Jen did, and they can do so quite easily.

WHY DORMANT EQUITY IS THE LAZIEST ASSET YOU CAN OWN

"Yep, I've got my house completely paid off," a guy I met at a dinner party recently bragged to me. Boy did he ever pick the wrong guy to say that to.

I thought about what to say back to him without being tactless. A million things rushed through my mind. I had case studies like Jen's in mind. I had facts, figures, and a thousand strong arguments.

Ultimately I just smiled and said politely, "I'd love to show you how to turn that into a productive asset. Give me a call if you're interested."

Because I realized something a long time ago — having a personal residence free and clear from mortgage might be one of the biggest financial blunders a modern Canadian could ever make, but people continue to do it anyways because it's a cultural narrative of our sensible middle class. And while it's not what I know to be the right financial decision, there is nothing wrong with playing it conservatively when you don't need to take risks. My passion for building wealth is not most people's prerogative.

Having said that, I do feel compelled, as always, to show the math. The fact is that a free and clear home simply means living in an expensive liability. A principal residence isn't actually an investment. It's a speculation at best, and a costly one at that. Once you factor in the cost of property taxes, maintenance, and the like, chances are you will come out financially behind where you would have if you were to rent. A principal residence is not an investment. It's a negative cash-flowing asset and thus an expense. You should always keep in mind that a principal residence's primary purpose is to provide shelter for you and your family. If it's your most valuable asset and you don't plan to liquidate it during your retirement, there is a decent chance your retirement plan is in trouble.

But living in a house you own does have the benefit of providing forced savings, and over a long enough time horizon it's likely that your wealth will grow due to appreciation and mortgage pay-down. Then your home becomes a haven for dormant equity. It sneaks in over the years, and many people don't know it's there. When you have a big chunk of dormant equity, you're aiding and abetting lazy money on your balance sheet.

I firmly believe people only do this because of the cultural narrative around having a free and clear property and the misunderstanding about the power of debt capital. Borrowing to invest in real estate provides debt capital in large quantities. I am also aware that, even though the math shows how powerful it is, many people prefer playing it safe.

I'm not trying to convince anyone who doesn't fit the risk tolerance profile of borrowing to invest. I'm just trying to show the way for those with the false beliefs of "common sense" and folk wisdom. If you have the risk tolerance for it, don't aid and abet lazy money on your balance sheet. Put it to work now and take advantage of the time value of money.

HOW REAL ESTATE MIMICS A PENSION FUND

Thirty years ago, almost a third of workers had great pensions. That was back in the retirement dream Valhalla of yesteryear, when defined benefit plans flowed throughout the land like water through the mountains — a time many will no doubt refer back to as the "good old days."

These days, it's more like 16 percent of workers who have great pensions.[22] That's a lot of lost retirements. As a result, we must take matters into our own hands to ensure a stable and secure retirement.

At times in this book we've emphasized the remarkable results that can be achieved when borrowing to invest in real estate. We know this action enables us to put multiple more dollars into the investment market even for the best savers amongst us. But the real power of the borrow-to-invest real estate retirement plan is that it provides a monthly coupon, which mimics a pension.

Take the example of Jen. Let's pretend the additional (nearly $4 million) in assets at the end of her twenty-five-year investment horizon didn't matter — which of course it does. Even in the extremely difficult-to-imagine event that the real estate market stayed flat for twenty-five years (which has never happened), Jen would still be in great shape for retirement at the end of her holding period. She would own two or three properties free and clear, and she would receive several thousand dollars per month in the form of rent cheques.

We don't need to spin a real-estate-riches story. The real — less sexy, but more important — story is that no other strategy creates a monthly coupon like real estate does. Bonds no longer provide a reliable monthly coupon. Add in the drying up of the pension wells, and you would have a potentially wretched situation for retirees — if it weren't for real estate. Real estate is the natural asset class to buy to offset failing pensions and the drop in bond returns. With only the anemic CPP and OAS benefits to see retirees through month to month, you can look to fix your monthly retirement income shortfall by sprucing up your resumé, or you can channel some of your assets (debt and equity capital) into real estate today to supplement your pension.

A client of mine — I'll call him Mike — is a savvy, smart guy who worked as CFO at a company that was sold. His work didn't provide a pension, so he realized early that he would need to create his own pension fund. Mike has received a couple of windfalls along the way — one from the sale of his company, and another from an inheritance. But Mike knew that he wouldn't be receiving those types of windfalls later in his life, post-career. He also knew that his savings alone wouldn't be enough to see him through the golden years, so he started crunching the numbers and looking around at his options. Being the smart financial guy that he is, Mike soon realized that borrowing to invest would allow him to buy real estate to act as a pension.

Then Mike set his plan in motion. He never sought real estate riches. In fact, he doesn't even buy for appreciation. Of course, appreciation happens regardless, but there are strategic ways to buy for more appreciation than less. It comes down to selecting markets more primed for appreciation than others.

In the Greater Toronto Area, properties within the city of Toronto generally appreciate faster than properties in some of the outlying areas, but the outlying areas can often have stronger cash flow. (Keep in mind that cash flow is typically at the expense of appreciation, which is a more tax-efficient builder of wealth.) Choosing between the two is a genuinely difficult decision for many investors. Do you want more cash flow or appreciation? It is very difficult to find a balance where both build simultaneously.

Mike chose to buy in some small towns outside of Toronto, towns that likely wouldn't be on most people's radar. While he has earned considerable cash flow, I will also point out that he has forfeited enormous appreciation along the way — which is a distinct trade-off. A trade-off he was willing to make, but certainly one to consider.

Mike uses a detailed but simple-to-learn analysis when buying properties. It can be summed up in this simple figure: 8 percent income. He looks for properties that earn 8 percent of the total value of the property in income each year. If he purchases a property for $500,000, it means the property would have to earn at least $40,000 in income. Then he has to deduct expenses, which vary from property to property. With that kind of income-to-purchase-price ratio, a well-planned purchase provides significant cash flow.

The key is to find a market where rents are sufficiently strong while at the same time having a low-enough purchase price. There is a sweet spot to be found in the outlying areas of most major centres. Keep in mind though that outlying areas tend to have less diversified economic bases than major cities, so while the cash flow may be greater, it may not be as stable. You would be very hard pressed to find a property with such strong cash flows in major cities, but you *can* still find positive cash flow.

Finding great cash-flowing deals, such as the ones Mike buys, can take a bit of time. You have to do the research and be patient for the right deal, and you will need a few connections, but it can be done. Working with a world-class real estate agent like Simon Giannini makes searching and negotiating far easier.

Mike typifies the practice of using real estate to create a monthly coupon. With the right team in place, you can make your real estate investments into exactly what you need them to be. For investors with longer time horizons, lower cash flow may be acceptable. The question is this: What monthly income do you need by what year? What amount of real-estate-derived income will stand in for a pension? From that initial assessment, simply work backwards to come up with your real estate retirement plan.

As always, the right team, starting with a world-class financial planner and real estate agent, will help you crunch the numbers to create the plan that's right for you.

RISK MITIGATION WHEN BORROWING TO INVEST IN REAL ESTATE

Mention the idea of borrowing to invest, and many folks' eyes flutter and their hearts palpitate. "That's risky," they might say.

It's one of the biggest paradoxes in our world today. Often the same people wouldn't bat an eye if a friend called them and said, "Hey, I just took out a bunch of home equity and got myself a new sports car." But if the same friend called them and said, "Hey, I just took out a bunch of home equity to invest because I fundamentally believe that the U.S. stock market is undervalued," or, "I fundamentally believe the forced savings of appreciable real estate assets is the way to go," many people would pause and reflect. They would — at minimum — think it's odd behaviour and would more likely think it's enormously risky.

We need to shift our paradigm. People should be concerned when their friends buy liabilities with borrowed money, while borrowing to buy appreciable assets should be cause to stop and think, "My friend is pretty smart."

The first step to mitigating the risk of borrowing money is to never borrow to buy liabilities. Beyond that, there are several powerful steps we can take to mitigate the risk of borrowing to invest. Some of the considerations we'll discuss apply to all types of borrowing to invest. Others apply only to investing in real estate.

Psychological Financial Risk Tolerance

Simply put, if you can't tolerate the ups and downs of investing financially and psychologically, then don't borrow to invest. Real estate investment markets go up and down, and you have to be mentally and financially comfortable with the worst-case scenario.

I would like to point out that overcoming this fear is largely the result of knowledge and understanding. If you look at many charts of major cities' real estate appreciation over time, you will notice that it looks like a mountain with jagged peaks everywhere. When you normalize the same chart and adjust out the peaks, though, the chart line suddenly looks more like the gentle slope of a hill, moving upwards slowly.

TORONTO MLS AVERAGE PRICE

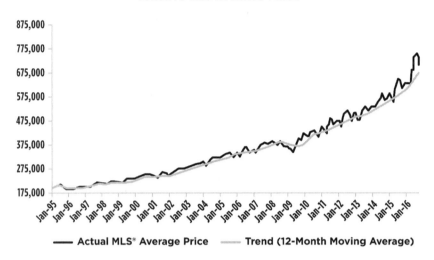

—— Actual MLS® Average Price   ——— Trend (12-Month Moving Average)

Source: Toronto Real Estate Board

Learning to invest and understanding market cycles is an important early step to take in financial literacy. With that said, based on the best knowledge and understanding available to you, the first step when making a decision whether to borrow to invest is to know your own risk tolerance. Only borrow to invest if you can mentally and psychologically handle market fluctuations.

Hold Cycle

If you don't have a long time horizon (a minimum of five years, but I strongly suggest ten or longer), then don't get in the game. If you may need to cash in early due to liquidity requirements or to fund your lifestyle, this is not a suitable strategy for you. If your window is too short, you run a much higher risk of getting caught in a down cycle. Five years is typically long enough to overcome a market lull, but having a ten-year investment horizon would all but guarantee it. There are no guarantees in any type of investment, but after ten years you will typically see strong growth. Make sure you can stay in the game long enough to profit without causing financial hardship in another area of life.

Interest Rates

What are current interest rates? Is your rate fixed or variable? What's the term of your investment? Don't rely on the math of short-term borrowing if you need it to make the numbers work in the long term.

I firmly believe that interest rates will stay low for the foreseeable future, but I don't do my long-term financial projections based on those low numbers. I calculate a worst-case scenario, where interest rates rise dramatically (using a 3 percent stress test). Only if my investments will still cover the cost of borrowing, after accounting for a sharp rise in rates, will I make an investment with borrowed funds.

Remember that it's actually the after-tax cost of borrowing that matters. Consider this: if you're in the 50 percent tax bracket, even a rise of interest rates to 6 percent would be equivalent to an after-tax cost of borrowing of 3 percent because you can deduct half of your interest expense in taxes. In other words, your leveraged money will still be profitable even if the investments you make with it only return just over 3 percent. Watch the after-tax numbers, not the surface rate of interest, when running the math.

Rates of Return

What are the expected and minimum rates of return? Like the cost of borrowing, it's the after-tax rate of return that matters. Your after-tax rate of return must be greater than your after-tax cost of borrowing or the financial math won't add up in your favour. Never leave this to guess work and always take the time to run the numbers.

We can't be certain of future returns, since they will fluctuate with the market, but, based on everything you know about the history of your investment type and the best advice of the professional team you employ, ask yourself what the average and worst-case scenarios look like. If you can't live with the worst-case scenario, don't move ahead with the investment.

Across Canada, real estate has returned on average 5.5 percent over the past thirty years. But perhaps you might be extremely unlucky and find yourself in a ten-year lull where the market returns only 3.5 percent. Keep this in mind (and stress-test for it) when deciding whether to borrow money to invest.

Making Payments on the Mortgage

Do you have enough flexibility in your budget or balance sheet to afford to make the payments on time even in your low-income months? Perhaps a tenant will miss paying rent, for example. If you don't have debt service space, then wait until you do. Get your financial house in better order, then proceed. When investing in real estate, you will have a (comparatively) high degree of certainty that all of your debt will be serviced based on income from the property. For additional security, though, start a reserve fund when purchasing the investment. This will cover any months the property doesn't earn income. To be even more certain, don't borrow to invest unless you know you could service the debt using only your regular income. Having to do so is a worst-case scenario, but an important one to consider.

If you have enough liquidity, in terms of savings, that it enables you to make payments in the event you have a vacancy or a surprise expense, then you're fine to go ahead and borrow to make the investment. If not, you're on a thin line and you should probably take a step back. Re-assess and improve your financial situation before proceeding.

Quality Tenant Selection

One of the greatest investor fears is that a tenant will destroy or at least cause significant damage to a property. The investor would be put in the unenviable position of having to repair the property at his or her own expense. This is a real concern, and quality property management will eliminate much of the risk. But here's the truth on this real estate bogeyman: it's highly unlikely to happen. Very rarely will your property be trashed in such a way as to not be covered by insurance. A worst-case scenario might mean having to continue making mortgage payments on the property (which would be taken care of by your reserve fund) while awaiting insurance money. However, such a situation wouldn't arise unless you had treated your tenants poorly in the first place, and that's just something a decent landlord would never do. Your tenants are looking after one of your most valuable assets, and so you should treat them with the greatest respect.

A more common, but still relatively rare, occurrence is for a tenant to stop paying rent. You might never recover those lost months' rent, but you can dramatically minimize the occurrence of this circumstance with quality tenant selection. You can also stop the bleeding by evicting the tenant as soon as legally allowed. A great property manager will do all this on your behalf.

These measures are simple. A few prudent steps will protect you in 95 percent of cases or more. Simply screen tenants by calling their prior landlords, checking their credit history to find out if they've missed many payments in the past, confirming their income, and having them fill out rental applications. Many landlords don't take these steps, which I suspect is where most real estate horror stories come from.

Reserve Funds

As mentioned previously, you will work your numbers based on your ability to cover the debt service expense even in months when cash flow is low. In other words, if you can't make the payments on a month when you earned no rental income, then don't borrow to invest in real estate.

Keep in mind that your own personal income is the third line of defence. First is the rental income from the property. Second is the reserve fund, which you will prepare before buying. The reserve fund is a separate bank account that you put a certain amount of money in when you purchase the property — often the equivalent of three months' rent. You will never allow the reserve fund to go below that amount, and in fact you will want to grow it. A great team will always advise you and remind you to build your reserve fund *before* buying.

Cash Flow Projections

Instead of simply keeping your reserve fund even at three months' rent, it's a good idea to funnel some of the additional cash flow toward an ever-growing reserve fund. Do a detailed analysis of a property to project future expenses so that you can use the cash flow from the property to fund future renovations in advance.

To do that, you must purchase a property with strong cash flow. Cash flow in real estate is typically defined as money earned by a property over and above its expenses. Cash flow projections vary wildly between types of property, the local market, the properties' expenses, and more. Typically we find that high-appreciation markets like Toronto have lower cash flow partly because when value goes up, rent controls prevent the rent from rising as fast. The trade-off is better appreciation. Strong cash-flowing markets make the most sense for investors looking to create a strong coupon that mimics a pension.

If there was ever anything to be detail-oriented about, it's this: don't buy a property unless you have a high degree of certainty about the cash-flow projections. Great cash flow can protect you from a lot of market turmoil and a number of other sins. Use the excess money the property throws off every month to mitigate risk.

Insurance

The only truly Armageddon-like event in real estate investing is an uninsured catastrophic loss of a property. The right kind of insurance completely eliminates this risk. Make sure you have it, and never borrow to invest unless you're a hundred percent certain you are insured against all realistically potential catastrophes.

This is an important point, because different properties will have different insurance requirements. The type of property, neighbourhood, and renter profile will define what type of insurance you need. Find a great insurance agent connection and learn the basics of rental real estate insurance.

Quality Team

In many ways, building a quality team is the master tip for any real estate investor, but especially the investor considering borrowing to invest. (Actually, having the best team possible in any situation will help you excel in life.) If you have the right team, they will inform you on each of the risk mitigation strategies I've mentioned and probably others.

Your financial planner will help you plan the purely financial risk mitigation strategies. Your mortgage professional will get you the best mortgage terms and conditions to support your long-term portfolio goals. Your real estate agent will help you select a neighbourhood and property type that will appreciate in value and collect cash flow. Your insurance agent will help cover your butt. Your property manager will select excellent tenants. Your accountant will minimize your tax expenses by calculating your tax deductions.

Building your team of trusted advisors and then heeding their advice is the best way to mitigate risk. Work only with people who are qualified and have a track record of delivering results in the area in which you are looking to invest.

CAN YOU ACCESS DORMANT EQUITY?

Answer the following questions to self-assess whether you could and should borrow money to invest in real estate:

- Do you own your own home?
- How long have you owned your home for?
- Has the market appreciated in your city or town since you purchased your home?
- Have you paid down a significant amount on your mortgage since you first purchased the home?
- Is your house "free and clear" of mortgage?
- Do you have the psychological and emotional make-up to withstand the pressure of market fluctuations?
- Are you willing to take the few simple but vital steps necessary to dramatically mitigate the risk of borrowing to invest?
- Could you benefit from putting many multiples more money in the market or do you need to do so to secure a stable retirement?
- Do you understand the benefit of using debt capital as much as equity capital?
- Could you benefit from adding a monthly income (coupon) that would mimic a pension fund in your retirement?

THE POWER OF BORROWING TO INVEST

I hope it has become blatantly obvious to you throughout this chapter how powerful (and relatively low-risk) borrowing to invest can be. My new friend at the dinner party, Mike, and Jen are all just regular people.

Jen is well on her way to creating an incredible retirement for herself even if she only does half as well as the scenario we laid out for her.

Mike is a smart guy who took action late in his working life (but not too late). Because his goal is a monthly coupon and because his investment horizon is still long enough, it makes sense for him to borrow to invest. As a result, his investments pay him a coupon that mimics a pension. He receives cheques every month.

My friend at the dinner party might one day see how much money he's leaving on the table. I can't say for sure. He hasn't called me yet. But what we can say about him for certain is this: when he retires, he'll have the value of his home on his balance sheet, along with whatever else he's created along the way, and that's not the worst thing in the world.

Maybe he's been an incredible saver. I'm not sure, but as we've seen from the many examples in this book already, it's difficult for anyone to be a good enough saver to do better than they would have by borrowing to invest.

Borrowing to invest in real estate requires a solid plan and preparation. It's not something to jump into hastily. You must have both psychological fortitude and your numbers in order. But the financial results that follow from a well-executed borrow-to-invest plan are powerful in comparison to typical personal finance results.

CHAPTER 7
Selecting a Mortgage Professional

Talent wins games, but teamwork and intelligence wins championships.
— MICHAEL JORDAN

A KEY TEAM MEMBER

Many mortgage providers are trained to write mortgages in a manner that allows them to complete the transaction for their clients. Their training is centred around deal thinking, which is appropriate when you consider that most Canadian consumers only own one home. This is a problem for investors, since selecting the incorrect mortgage on the first property can disqualify the investor from securing further mortgages on subsequent properties, or at least set them back in the long term.

If the mortgage professional doesn't understand the long-term strategy of borrowing to invest, the foundations of financial planning, and the individual client's specific goals and needs, the chances of long-term success are low.

More common, though, is the mortgage professional who simply puts clients into any old mortgage without proper planning. These mortgage professionals are transaction-focused instead of relationship-focused. Short-term thinking causes long-term problems much of the time. Thus, it is vitally important to select a qualified mortgage professional who focuses on investment real estate and understands the investor's wish to use borrowed money to invest in multiple properties. Formal financial-planning training is also a critical component of being able to advise effectively.

Even with this planning in place, things can still get tricky. Individuals who have a goal of retiring prosperously using real estate as their path must carefully plan purchases. The greatest asset you might have for achieving this goal is a mortgage professional who fully understands your dreams and has an established track record of delivering the same results for other clients.

THE NEED FOR AN INVESTMENT SPECIALIST MORTGAGE PROFESSIONAL

The problem with most people's relationships with mortgage professionals is that they don't have one. They see a mortgage as a transaction and think, "Why would I stay in touch with my mortgage broker for years after purchasing my home if I'm not planning on purchasing another home?"

A person buying only a personal residence, with no other financial goals, might only interact with a mortgage professional every five years. You might go to him or her when your mortgage term is expiring because you might want to shop around for a new mortgage. But even that is the rare person. More commonly, people will simply accept their bank's offer and continue with the same exact mortgage for another term.

Active real estate investors need to develop a great relationship with the right kind of mortgage professional. This person's advice, moral fortitude, and work ethic might be the greatest asset in your real-estate-investing arsenal. Conversely, choosing the wrong type of mortgage professional might hold you back enormously on your real estate path.

Imagine you had a borrowing portfolio of $200,000 invested with a financial planner. It's a serious commitment to give that much money to someone. Now imagine having $1 million in a borrowing portfolio. It's significantly more, and if you were researching which financial planner to use, you would (hopefully) do a significant amount of due diligence to make sure you were selecting the right kind of financial planner.

The exact same strategy should be used in the mortgage world. Once you step into the world of real estate investment, you want to put a significant amount of effort into selecting your mortgage professional, someone who's actually specializing in real estate investment borrowing. In fact, such a specialist isn't really just a mortgage professional. They must understand estate planning. Even more importantly, they must pro-actively manage the debt side of your portfolio.

How can you assess whether you've got the right kind of mortgage professional? I'll provide some questions that will help you qualify a mortgage professional later in this chapter, but I'd like to share with you the key sign you've found a great one and the type of relationship you should expect with a world-class mortgage professional once you become a real estate investor. If they are competent enough to be a mortgage professional for an investor like you, he or she will start off by asking, "What's your goal?"

A poorly planned early mortgage, not beginning with the end in mind, will affect later mortgages negatively. You don't want your mortgage profes-sional to look after the debt side of a portfolio transaction-by-transaction, only to find out later that you've missed the mark on your actual goals. So a mortgage professional who is serious about helping you plan for the long term will first ask why you're picking real estate as an asset.

In our office, if someone approaches real estate as a get-rich-quick scheme, we politely tell them we're not a good fit and refuse to proceed with serving them. We get excited if they tell us that they're in it for the forced savings mechanism or that they love the fact it's a hedge against inflation, or better yet that they're going to use real estate to fund retirement goals as part of a well thought-out, long-term finan-cial plan. We're looking for clients who are thinking long-term, just as you should be looking for a mortgage professional who is thinking long-term. The moment we know we have a committed client who truly gets the long-term power of real estate, but who isn't looking for magic, get-rich-quick-type results, we start helping them plan.

The first thing we need to know is whether they have done any budget-ing or cash-flow planning. This enables us to understand how much money they will need during retirement. Most people have the goal to "build wealth," but this phrase has drastically different meanings for everyone.

Most people think "financially successful" means having a paid-off mortgage before retirement and being able to take a vacation once or twice a year, eat out on occasion, and not worry about money during retirement. Others might have bigger dreams, like sailing around the world in retire-ment and quitting work much younger. On the other end of the spectrum are the people with the lowest expectations, who think they will have to "downsize" at retirement just to survive through the last years of their life.

Great mortgage professionals will ask you a series of questions to determine what you want before looking at anything else. If they're doing their job right, this early work will help them identify if perhaps your plan and your idea to get there might be incorrect.

At times we've found clients who believe they need to purchase one rental property in order to reach their retirement goals, when in reality it will require two or three to realize their dreams. But more commonly we see clients who believe their dreams will be enormously expensive and require a massive portfolio of real estate. These clients are then happy to learn the truth — that reaching their goals will likely require only a handful of properties.

ACTIVELY MANAGING YOUR DEBT PORTFOLIO

One of the most important roles that a mortgage professional must play in order to help you achieve your goals is to actively manage debt and show you how to use debt intelligently to optimize longer-term household cash flow and wealth-maximization goals. But what exactly does that mean? First, as mentioned, the mortgage professional must understand your goals. But the primary job of your mortgage professional once he or she knows your goals is to make sure you *always have access to capital* so long as you want to continue investing.

Access to capital is the key difference between a major REIT (real estate investment trust) and an individual investor. The big institutional investors can always raise capital, but many individuals can't. It's the prime obstacle people face when building wealth.

In personal finance you really need only two things to create wealth. First, you need to spend less money than you make. If you don't do that, you won't have any capital to begin with or the debt service numbers required to secure a mortgage.

Second, you need to be able to deploy the limited amount of capital you have left (debt or equity) in its highest and best use. Capital is always scarce, and since you need capital to create wealth, your mortgage professional's ability to manage your debt capital becomes vital. Access to capital is the name of the game in real estate. As you've seen throughout this book, leveraging capital is the way to build wealth, so it stands to reason that the biggest impediment to wealth creation is lack of access to capital.

The banks love to lend you money on real estate, but at the same time they have a low risk tolerance. They want to know that if there is trouble in your portfolio you will still be able to make your mortgage payments. This becomes a bigger problem for investors looking to expand their portfolios. The more properties you have, the more difficult it becomes to borrow money. Few lenders will be willing to lend to you. If you want to have a reasonable chance of getting financing on properties six, seven, and eight, you will need to save your easy approvals for the end. But people typically follow the path of least resistance early in their investing journey. They go to their local bank and use up the easy approvals first.

You should do it in the exact opposite way. Later in your real estate investing career you should go where you have the most negotiating power and the most leverage to do your more difficult loans. The reasoning behind this is simple. If you have a chequing account, RRSPs, TFSAs, RESPs, and a credit card there, then the bank will be a bit more mindful about letting you walk out the door and take your mortgage elsewhere. You simply have more leverage — leverage to get leverage — at your own bank, so you should save it for later purchases, when you might need it.

When your debt portfolio is being mismanaged, you will find that the financing runs out very quickly. Poor debt service numbers can cause this. The mortgage professional's job is to minimize your payments for qualification purposes. To see how this works, go to www.realestateretirementplan.ca to download a payment optimization chart.

Another key component in managing your debt financing comes down to choosing the right mortgage product. To ensure ongoing access to more funds, the mortgage professional should help you select a mortgage that lets you refinance as the principal is paid down and the property appreciates. Remember Lucy? This exact mortgage strategy is how she was able to create such significant wealth. We planned her mortgages so that she could continue to pull more equity out of new properties as it became available. As a result, she never ran out of debt capital to finance the next purchase. We also ensured that her payments remained below a certain threshold so that she could qualify for the next property.

INTERVIEWING A MORTGAGE PROFESSIONAL

To assist you in your search for a world-class mortgage professional, I've put together a list of ten questions to ask a prospective mortgage professional before hiring them. Below each question are guidelines that will help you assess their answers.

If they can answer these questions to your satisfaction, then you are likely in capable hands, but make sure you ignore sales pitches and stick to provable facts. This simple list of questions will help you quickly determine how legitimate their expertise is.

1) **Every mortgage person presents him or herself as an expert in the area of mortgage finance. Can you tell me about your educational background and the experience you have in this area?**
   Unfortunately, the barrier to entry into the mortgage industry is low, so this is an important question. Ideally your mortgage professional should have credentials in finance: a combination of post-secondary education and any relevant designations. Some useful degrees and designations are a BA in economics, a B.Comm or BBA (ideally in finance), an MBA (ideally in finance), a Certified Financial Planner (CFP), or a Personal Financial Planner (PFP). Real estate investing is an estate-planning play, so using someone who doesn't have formal financial planning training is just not sensible.

2) **How many mortgages have you personally arranged in your career?**
   While your prospect doesn't have to be among the top mortgage professionals in the country, you also don't want your mortgage financing transaction to be their training course. I would not consider working with someone who has arranged fewer than 250 mortgages.
   I would also be reluctant to work with someone who funds less than one hundred mortgages a year, because it means they aren't doing enough business to keep on top of the changing market conditions. If someone is great at what they do, they will be sought after and their results will reflect this.

3) **How many properties do your top three real estate investment clients own?**
   The answer to this question provides you with two key pieces of information. First, it confirms how established some of their real estate investment clients are without you having to reveal how many properties you plan to buy. Second, you now know if they have a track record of helping people with your target number of properties.
   It is easy for a mortgage professional to have done mortgage loans for someone with a second home or one investment property, but a much different skill set is required to serve investors who have a vast and complicated group of real estate holdings spread among multiple ownership structures.

4) **Can you give me three personal references from people you've helped finance over ten properties for?**
   This simple question will help you differentiate between the sales person and the true real estate investment mortgage specialist. If they can't provide written references upon request, then they are not qualified to do the job.
   Lots of people misrepresent their track record, but any mortgage professional who has been honest will see this as an opportunity to validate the facts they have presented and will gladly put you in touch with clients who will vouch for their professionalism and expertise.

5) **Where does the majority of your business come from?**

If most of the mortgage professional's business comes from satisfied client referrals and repeat customers, this speaks to a high level of customer satisfaction. If most of their business comes from referrals, then they will be happy to provide references.

6) **What systems or procedures do you have in place to look after my mortgages?**

Keeping accurate client records, as well as providing consistent and accurate market updates and reports on changing market conditions, is a key part of a long-term relationship with a mortgage professional. It's cause for concern if they don't have a way to look after you beyond the closing date of the mortgage. To succeed in real estate investing, you need a relationship, not transaction advice.

7) **How will bond yields affect mortgage rates?**

This is perhaps the most basic mortgage rate movement question, and it should prompt a two-part answer. The first part of the answer should include the fact that bond yields affect fixed mortgage rates only. The second part should state that when bond yields go up, they put upward pressure on fixed mortgage rates. This is a very basic question, and a person who can't answer it doesn't understand the mortgage market.

8) **What is the most common reason the Bank of Canada increases interest rates?**

The bank is focused on inflation as its target. In general, inflation should fall between 1 and 3 percent. When inflation starts to go higher than 2 percent, the Bank of Canada considers tightening (raising rates). Conversely, if it's lower than 2 percent, the bank considers stimulation (lowering rates). This question should be as simple as asking someone their last name. If the mortgage professional doesn't know the answer, run away!

9) **What kind of books, seminars, or training do you use to keep current?**

A top mortgage professional will have a systematic approach to keeping on top of market conditions. If they don't have a plan and a clear list of sources they use for their data, then the credibility of their knowledge may be subject to debate.

Being a true market expert doesn't happen by accident, and an individual can become a licensed mortgage specialist with as little as forty hours of training in some provinces. Lifelong learning is required to keep you on top of your game.

10) **Would you suggest I compare your mortgage advice to that of others?**

The mortgage agent should not only be comfortable with this suggestion, but also encourage it. The agent should feel confident in his or her ability and how it compares to others.

Life is too short to deal with average service providers. The cost of doing business this way could literally be not achieving your retirement goals. Use these questions to qualify your mortgage professional.

Of course, I would put my team and myself against anyone else in the industry, anywhere in Canada. Furthermore, we can handle mortgages for clients across the country. Please feel free to contact us through our website, www.mortgagemanagement.ca.

THE POWER OF A GREAT MORTGAGE PROFESSIONAL

As I hope has become obvious throughout the first six chapters of this book, borrowing to invest might be the one tried-and-true method for average Canadians to create a strong retirement and generational wealth. Reaching your retirement goals requires ongoing access to capital at the moment you most need it. Bringing the wrong mortgage professional onboard your team could sabotage the mission of creating the retirement you desire.

The same can be said about a financial planner and a real estate agent. In Chapter 4, I provided a framework for selecting a financial planner, and now you've got everything you need to find a world-class mortgage professional. Remember that what you need most is a strong team, but you will also need ongoing education. The knowledge and action plan you can put together based on the information in this book is a good start. In Part 3, which follows, Simon Giannini will discuss the more real-estate-specific teachings that will get you started on your real estate retirement plan.

PART 3

Real Estate — More Powerful than Any Other Asset Class

CHAPTER 8
How to Profit from Real Estate
by Simon Giannini

> Real estate investing, even on a very small scale, remains a tried and true means of building an individual's cash flow and wealth.
>
> — ROBERT KIYOSAKI

HOW DOES REAL ESTATE WORK?

So far in this book, Calum has spoken broadly about real estate, and in doing so has laid the groundwork and answered the important questions about how real estate can fit into an overall retirement and investment plan. He has shared some numbers from client success stories and the lack of numbers (the profit) from people who have failed to invest. Many new investors find it hard to believe, but you don't actually need a huge amount of your own cash to get started in real estate. But you do need access to some form of capital, and thankfully, due to the mortgages and lenders in the market today, new investors (and all investors) have more access to capital than ever before.

Which is why this book is so important. It addresses the biggest problem of real estate investing and shows the solution for overcoming it: namely, that many folks have the money, sitting right there in their homes unused as dormant equity, and all they need to access it is to recognize that it's riskier not to.

But once new investors get past the fear and misunderstanding about their ability to access money, they still need to understand the mechanics of real estate. Putting together a world-class real estate team will take away most of your concerns, but a team is only as good as its leader. You must be the leader of your real estate team. That might sound a bit scary, but it shouldn't be. It doesn't mean you have to be some kind of battle-hardened boss. It just means you must be educated and lead your team.

As the leader of your real estate team, you need to have vision and know where you're pointing your financial ship. The ideas and teachings in this book can give you very good ideas. Add your own retirement dreams into the mix with your new-found knowledge and you will have the beginnings of a plan. Your team will help you hone your plan, adding the missing pieces and showing you the steps that might still be a little fuzzy to you.

As the leader of your real estate team, you also need to be conversant in all things real estate. In the next three chapters I'll discuss all of the fundamental concepts you will need to bring your knowledge and vision in line with your knowledge of the retirement problem, financial planning, and borrowing to invest. In this chapter, we'll discuss how exactly real estate works. I've touched on it in earlier chapters, but I'll discuss it in more detail here. I'll show you exactly how the mechanism of real estate profit works and why I believe it's the most tried and true path to creating the sustainable wealth available to most Canadians.

Of course, real estate should be an important part of a broader portfolio of investments, not the only investment. But the situation we have in Canada tilts more toward the opposite problem. People have their RRSPs invested in mutual funds only. They fail to own cash-producing real estate and thereby miss out on its benefits. As part of your strategy, you should consult a financial planning expert to figure out what portfolio mix best suits your specific situation.

Some have described real estate as a four-course meal. In other words, there are four ways to profit from real estate. I've mentioned the first three already, so I'll summarize them. The first is mortgage pay-down. Regardless of anything else that happens in the real estate market, you can rely on your real estate investments to reliably pay down your mortgage. As the mortgage is paid down, your equity goes up.

Second is cash flow. Once all of your property expenses have been paid, the money remaining is your cash flow. There are some investment markets in which cash flow is so strong that even without any of the other ways to profit, investors are creating pension-mimicking cash flows with only a couple of properties.

Third is appreciation. We cannot rely on appreciation from one year to the next because we have no control over it. The market dictates whether it goes up or down. However, we have incredibly strong historical proof showing that the real estate market rises gently over time. We'll discuss how and why that happens in this chapter.

The fourth profit centre is forced appreciation. Part of the value of any real estate property is the condition of the building or buildings on the property. When it comes to valuing a property, the solution is always somewhat subjective. The value comes down to what someone is willing to pay for it.

When we're talking about investment properties, people are willing to pay a certain amount based on the income the property makes. Properties that are renovated to a certain modern standard earn more income. This could be cosmetic and, therefore, lead to higher-quality tenants desiring the property, or it could be structural and, therefore, change the use of the property (from one suite to two, for example). Forced appreciation refers to all the ways we are able to force up the value through renovations on the property.

But the master principle at play behind the power of real estate is leverage, and I'll reiterate its power in this chapter.

How can we be certain we'll profit in real estate? The hard answer is that we can never be one hundred percent certain. Nothing is certain in the investing world, but the same could be said for mutual funds and stock market investments. What we do know is that doing nothing will lead to no result. This do-nothing approach is the reason so many people are selling their principal residence or, worse yet, taking out reverse mortgages to fund their retirement.

MORTGAGE PAY-DOWN

We can't be certain of any investment strategy, but we can have a high degree of confidence that we'll profit from real estate so long as we invest and never speculate. Most horror stories (where folks lose money) come from speculation, which means buying purely with the hopes that the value might go up.

The same slow wealth-building principle works with investment real estate properties as with owner-occupied homes. You make the payments month after month, and it acts as a forced savings mechanism, building wealth slowly. Most Canadians use a mortgage to purchase their home and learn about the power of leverage accidentally. Borrowing funds enables them to slowly build equity every month as their mortgage shrinks. But the main difference when it comes to an investment property is that the tenant is paying into your forced savings mechanism, rather than those funds coming out of your own income.

If you look at a $400,000 mortgage over a twenty-five-year term at 3 percent, you will end up with an additional $10,939 of equity at the end of the first year of ownership as your monthly principal payments accrue. On the same loan, the bank will make $11,777 in interest by the time the first year of the loan comes to an end. The percentage of the monthly payment that goes toward principal grows every year, which is another reason why holding a property long-term is beneficial.

There are a couple of ways to look at the return on the mortgage pay-down. First, you can analyze it against the total value of the property. A $400,000 mortgage (at 80 percent loan-to-value) means you own a $500,000 property. In this case, $11,000 is more than a 2 percent return on investment. But if we only use the down payment component of your investment ($80,000) to calculate ROI, we're talking about a nearly 14 percent return. Either way, mortgage pay-down is a powerful force. It's a good deal all around. The tenant gets a great place to live. You get nearly $11,000 plus the opportunity to participate in other ROI plays — appreciation and cash flow.

The great thing about mortgage pay-down is that it sneaks up on you. It's not much use to you until it reaches a certain amount, and then it only becomes useful when you transform it from boring old dormant equity into useful investment capital. Mortgage pay-down takes advantage of the human tendency toward inertia. Once you've purchased a property, you begin earning a return by doing nothing. Since the gains are locked away, you're rarely tempted to use them to frivolous ends.

This is a major strategy point of this book and the reason you will need a world-class mortgage professional in your corner. We know that you will eventually unlock the $11,000 earned in mortgage pay-down — likely once a few years accrue and you've built up much more than $11,000 to fund another purchase. Hopefully — if it fits your plan — you'll do it multiple times.

Imagine the following scenario: You find out that you have $200,000 of dormant equity in your principal residence. Working with Calum, or someone like him, you could turn that dormant equity into the down payment on two separate rental properties, each worth $500,000. Twenty percent of $500,000 is $100,000. You would put down 20 percent on each property using the dormant equity in your home, while borrowing the remaining $400,000 to purchase each property. Then your investment specialist real estate agent would do a detailed analysis of each property to ensure they are solid investments that would earn you enough cash to cover all the expenses, with some positive cash flow remaining at the end.

Now you have two mortgages exactly like the first one we discussed at a rate of 3 percent interest assuming a twenty-five year amortization. This means that after the first year you would have built up nearly $22,000 in equity from the mortgage pay-down. At the end of the second year you would have built up more than $44,000. After year three, that figure grows to more than $67,000. By year four the combined new equity wealth in your portfolio from mortgage pay-down only (on both properties) would be more than $91,000.

Now you suddenly have a big chunk of equity available that you can leverage again. So, even if nothing else positive happens during that time (the market is flat or your cash flow is zero), you will still be in a position to purchase another property if it's in the plan.

Of course, chances are that the market would appreciate in that time. By actively managing your portfolio, we would ensure you're well positioned to capitalize once again. This is exactly what you would do if a few things were true: First, that you fit the risk profile of using debt capital to grow wealth. Second, that you're following the principle of highest and best use (you want to maximize your limited cash). Third, that it fits with your investment and retirement goals.

You may decide that two real estate investments are all you ever want to own. So you may decide to invest your new-found debt capital in a different asset class altogether or just leave the equity in the property and watch the cash flow increase. This is where a financial planner will play a vital role. Regardless of what you do with this additional capital, the point remains that mortgage pay-down is the consistent, predictable wealth creation principle of investment real estate. You can rely on it even when and if the other forms of wealth creation don't work.

CASH FLOW

Next, I'll tell you about one of my clients (I'll call him Paul) who had a very powerful approach to cash flow. But first let's just get clear about what cash flow is. It's the money (earned by the property) left over after all of the property's expenses have been paid.

The income of the property must be enough to cover your finance cost plus expenses, including tax, maintenance, and in some cases property management, plus repairs and upkeep. And, to be extra certain, we want to budget for vacancy and still add money to our contingency fund each month. On top of all that, you may want to take some cash and put it in your pocket. This is your cash flow, after all. If creating a monthly coupon is one of your main goals, then you will want a significant amount.

Here's a simple rule without exception: you never invest in cash-flow-negative properties. At the minimum your property needs to make you more money than it costs. You might think break-even cash flow doesn't sound like much of a good deal, but due to mortgage pay-down, market appreciation, and forced appreciation, we find consistently that even break-even properties end up being highly profitable over time.

It takes a certain type of property to produce positive cash flow. Your dream mansion in West Vancouver or the Bridle Path in Toronto won't be cash flow positive. The cost of the property and the relatively low income from renting it ensure that you would never be able to earn positive cash flow on such properties unless you purchased them with little to no financing.

Approaches to Cash Flow

We know that we need to have positive cash flow to survive and stay in the real estate game. Plus, real-estate cash flow can be a perfect stand-in for the monthly pension cheque that most people are no longer getting.

But just how much cash flow do you want and need? That's a question that completely depends on your financial goals and time horizon. Many investors in the peak earning years of their life often choose to forego large cash flows in favour of market appreciation.

Having more leverage across a portfolio lowers cash flow, but if you're leveraging for the right reasons — buying investments rather than liabilities — you will be participating in more market appreciation. It's a trade-off to carefully consider. By putting the emphasis on market appreciation instead of cash flow, you also minimize your tax exposure in the immediate term because you'll be receiving more capital gains. Capital gains are deferred until you realize the gain when you sell. Furthermore, only half of capital gains are taxable, but cash flow is treated like any normal income. So a potentially negative thing you can do from a tax perspective for someone in the top tax bracket — who is also in the prime earning years of his or her career — is to add a bunch more highly taxable income. Although many people would say that you would be lucky to have such a problem.

But, at a later stage of life, when the investor wants passive income from his or her investments to fund lifestyle, then it makes sense to earn more cash flow. This is the retirement coupon.

When investing in rental properties, we can actually "adjust the volume knob" on cash flows and leverage levels. This gives real estate investors a high level of control.

How to Achieve Positive Cash Flow

The answer to how to achieve positive cash flow is remarkably easy. The purpose of this book isn't to go into great detail on the finer points of cash flow, but it's worth mentioning quickly in a way that will stick with you.

If you can add and subtract (with or without a calculator), you can do cash flow projections. You start with the income a property earns, which typically comes from rent only, although some properties have additional sources of income, like laundry, parking, and storage rentals. Once you know your total income figure, you need to subtract all of the expenses. This includes principal and interest on mortgages, insurance, property tax, management fees, maintenance fees, reserve funds, and in some cases utilities. We'll cover each of those in more detail in the next chapter when we talk about expenses.

But that's how simple it is to calculate and predict cash flow. A little bit of addition and a little bit of subtraction is all it takes. Finding out the true numbers for each income and expense is easy. An investment specialist real estate agent like me will be able to help you find the exact or near exact figures on all your numbers.

Willful ignorance is a bigger problem that some new investors face than calculating cash flow or finding exact numbers. Or perhaps a better way to say it would be "hopeful ignorance." New investors can be in such a hurry to get started investing that they will tell themselves convenient lies to justify a purchase. Again, the right team members on your side can be a saving grace. They will question your number projections and intervene when you are looking at your potential investment through rose-coloured glasses.

A world-class real estate agent, mortgage professional, or financial planner will be relationship-focused, not transaction-focused. They will know that by helping you purchase a great property (not just any property) with strong cash flow numbers, they will benefit themselves in the long term because you'll come back to them to buy your next property. Thus, they will intervene where necessary. But if you act bravely and speak the truth to yourself, you won't need your team's intervention because you will not fudge the cash flow numbers just to make a deal.

Paul's Retirement Story

Paul is a long-time client of mine who typifies how to change the volume levels on cash flow and leverage. He's adjusted them depending on the stages of his life, career, and earning potential. Today, as Paul looks toward the next twenty years, his only goal is to maintain the lifestyle he currently has.

Paul started investing several years ago when he owned a condo in downtown Toronto. At the time he loved his job but wanted more money. He saw early on the problem that we're discussing in this book. He didn't have a pension. He knew that the CPP and what he'd managed to scrape together in RRSP investments wouldn't take him very far. But he also knew that he had equity in his condo. Over the years it had appreciated significantly and he'd faithfully paid down the mortgage. The combination of the two meant he had a big chunk of dormant equity.

He decided to turn his equity into an investment. Paul knew he wanted simplicity in his life. He looked around at the best available investment options that would maximize simplicity and still be a strong investment, and he decided on buying another condo in his building.

At that time, Paul wasn't so focused on cash flow. There were better cash-flowing real estate investments available. Multiplexes, for example, typically earn stronger cash flows, especially when they are purchased outside of the downtown Toronto area. But Paul wanted simplicity. He wanted to be able to walk down the hall and collect his rent cheques.

Paul's first property quickly appreciated as he paid down the mortgage. So he bought another one. Then another. And another. As of today, he owns twenty condos, all in the same area.

Now, I almost hesitate to tell you this story because of the number of units he owns. It really depends on your goals and retirement dreams, but not everyone will need to own that many properties. Paul's plan wouldn't work for many. For example, most investors probably wouldn't want to buy twenty units if they were in buildings spread out across a large city, creating a logistical nightmare. It worked for Paul because he was able to buy all his properties in the same area. Each investor will need their own tailor-made plan, but that's okay because we can create a real estate retirement plan that works for anyone. You just need the help of your team to do so.

Paul used a higher amount of leverage in the first few years as he built up his portfolio, but today he's nearing retirement, and over the years he's lowered the leverage. Today he carries about 50 percent debt across the entire portfolio. This means that his mortgage payments are much lower, so his cash flow is much higher. Today, after paying all of his various mortgage payments each month, plus all of the other expenses, Paul is making about $500 of positive cash flow on each property. That means he's earning about $10,000 per month of positive cash flow across his entire portfolio. It's the ultimate security for a retiring person, because even if two tenants didn't pay rent on time, Paul would still have plenty of positive cash flow to deal with that shortfall.

Having several properties is actually a great risk mitigation strategy when your excess cash flow is enough to pay for potential lost income from tenants missing rent. This matters in theory. But in reality, Paul's tenants rarely miss paying rent. It might happen once every couple of years. He knows them all by name. They live under the same roof, and he's chosen an upscale area as his investment target. His tenants are well-selected from an already solid pool of potential. His portfolio is easily manageable. He's turning over maybe two or three units per year, but many of his tenants have been there eight, nine, ten, or fifteen years. Paul doesn't increase his rents as aggressively as he could, so he keeps very loyal tenants. Because remember, although he is very much focused on cash flow, Paul also places a high value on simplicity. Keeping good tenants happy for many years in a row is a great strategy for simplicity.

Paul adjusted the financing levers and knobs to put himself in this strong cash flow position so that he could live the retirement lifestyle he envisioned. He's hired a part-time property manager to take care of things when he's away, and while he's there, he hires outside help for every type of renovation.

Paul loves to travel and enjoys looking at his bank account balance online at the beginning of each month, when his bank balance inflates with the incoming rent cheques. It's a monthly ritual he often partakes in while overlooking a beach somewhere warm.

But even though he's cash-flow focused, let's take a look at the other components of his real estate profit centres. The average value of each of Paul's condos is around $500,000, which means that his total portfolio value is around $10 million. First of all, he isn't being taxed on the $10 million worth of real estate he owns because he's not selling it, so he hasn't realized a capital gain. The value of his portfolio continues to go up every year as he issues rent increases.

He keeps his portfolio about 50 percent financed, so he carries about $5 million in debt. It sounds like a huge amount, but with Paul's positive cash flow and the security it provides, the debt is the least of his concerns. Every year his tenants pay down more than $100,000 on his debt (3 percent average mortgage over twenty-five-year amortization), so his equity is still growing, even in a flat market. If he were earlier in his own personal financial life cycle, he would probably want to continue using that growing equity to purchase more real estate. But he won't do that now, since he's focused on positive cash flow as a pension replacement.

A common scenario I find amongst my clients is that they want $10,000 of passive income for their retirement, as Paul has. Once I know what their goals are, I can show them how to get there with the help of their real estate team. It depends on their ability to access capital, either debt or equity, and their borrowing power. They need to be able to qualify for loans. *Your own* personal real estate retirement plan is available to you. We simply need to start from the end and work backwards to create the plan. Many Canadians find themselves in the same position as Paul. They don't necessarily have the cash available, but they have significant equity in their personal residence.

Paul refinanced his condo and pulled out the money to buy his first. He was nervous, but he bought the first one. Over the years he used his own cash where necessary, but more often than not he would dip back into his debt capital to purchase another property. There were years when he would visit his mortgage broker only to find out that he had enough capital available to buy three more condos. He always bought with the minimum of 20 percent down and his portfolio was always solid and healthy.

Paul built one little golden goose, and from that golden goose he leveraged it into his retirement. Because he understood how to tweak the dials on his leverage and cash flow, Paul built his system exactly the way he needed it to be. In essence, he built his own powerful pension.

MARKET APPRECIATION

Wise investors don't rely on or expect appreciation in the short term. However, over the medium to long term, appreciation almost always creates the greatest wealth. In fact, it's not uncommon for appreciation to create many more multiples than mortgage pay-down or cash flow.

Let's take a look at Paul's portfolio, for example. He owns about $10 million worth of real estate. We already know he does well on both cash flow and mortgage pay-down, but how much will he earn on market appreciation? We can't know how much appreciation he will earn in any one year. Sometimes there is no appreciation. Other times it's strong. Most often it's average. But here's what we do know: in the past thirty years in Toronto, Paul's market, housing has gone up on average more than 5 percent every year.

It's true that there have been some multi-year lulls in that time. There's a chance that a multi-year lull might start right now. In that case, Paul's portfolio would not grow for a while. He doesn't care because he's not selling, but it's important for investors (especially new investors) to know that a market lull is possible. Don't invest, especially with borrowed money, unless you have a long enough time horizon to see through the entire market lull — typically five years is enough time.

But, in the past, the Toronto market has appreciated on average 5.5 percent annually.[23] For ease of math, let's call it 5 percent. On his portfolio of $10 million, this would equate to pre-tax earnings of $500,000. On market appreciation alone! We must always think in terms of after-tax dollars, though. If indeed Paul were to sell (because only then are capital gains taxed), he would be looking at a hefty tax bill. Of course, some years his portfolio would depreciate, but in those years he would still earn cash flow and mortgage pay-down.

This situation well describes how every investor should act, regardless of where they are in the life cycle of their investments. Always take care of cash flow and mortgage pay-down first. Plan your investments to be profitable even if your portfolio doesn't appreciate. Then, when the market appreciates, you get a nice doubling of returns. The good news is that, over time, history shows us that chances are this will happen. But if a single year doesn't earn you a return, the average over a longer period of time almost certainly will. I challenge you to find me a ten-year moving average in which it would have been a bad time to invest. It doesn't exist.

But it only works if you can stay invested. You have to be able to ride out the market lulls. The worst thing to do is sell just at the most inopportune moment.

Predicting Market Appreciation

Everything we discussed about appreciation won't matter if you purchase in the entirely wrong city, region, or neighbourhood. Your local region might not even be a good investing spot.

Across Canada, as a whole, our real estate markets are full of strong performers. However, it's important never to let national averages guide your decision to invest. Even in an overall strongly performing real estate nation like Canada, there are poor-performing pockets. It's important that you understand the economic fundamentals of the region you're looking to invest in before you invest. The same things that drive real estate market growth also drive the country's economic growth.

Will there be more people moving into the region? Is there growth in jobs? Is the average income of the local residents going up? What is the vacancy rate? Then there are more neighbourhood-specific indicators. Is your property close to amenities? What do the surrounding properties look like? What is the crime rate in your area? Both the regional and neighbourhood indicators are absolutely vital to predicting whether your neighbourhood is likely to appreciate. If there is strong demand in the present and the foreseeable future, then real estate is likely to appreciate in the area.[24] If not, then it's best to take a pass. Often when beginning to invest, the best market is the one you live in, due to the simplicity of managing and sourcing properties. In cases where the values may drop for many years in the future, though, it's best to avoid your home region. However, if the long-term outlook is stable (but not appreciating rapidly), you may still want to invest near home and simply make it a mortgage pay-down and cash-flow play.

Educate yourself on the best possible strategy for you and the options available in your target regions. Always get the best advice available from a team of experts.

FORCED APPRECIATION

Another strategy that's often treated as completely separate is to force appreciation on a property through targeted renovations. We've all heard about house flippers. This term usually refers to people who buy, fix, and immediately sell.

I wouldn't recommend selling quickly. The main benefits of real estate take time to accrue: cash flow doesn't come unless you put renters in the property, mortgage pay-down piles up over the course of years, and market appreciation is a glacial force that can no more be stopped than the rising and falling of tides. The house flipper misses out on all of these and attempts to force appreciation quickly and then sell for an immediate profit. All of this income is taxed as regular income, and in practice flipping doesn't often work well.

But we can take one positive lesson from flippers: the idea of forcing appreciation. This is the most active way to grow wealth in real estate and, as such, comes with a set of benefits and drawbacks. Ultimately, you may decide that forcing appreciation is not your cup of tea. But what I often find is that after real estate investors complete their first one or two deals, they lose the fear of what might happen and start to see a world of possibility. By calculating the expenses and potential benefits of forcing appreciation, just as you would any other part of the deal, investors soon discover that forcing appreciation often makes perfect sense.

If you could create $20,000, $50,000, $80,000, or $100,000 of additional capital just by managing a month-long renovation project, wouldn't you consider it? Again, this strategy isn't for everyone, and everything we said about having a team becomes twice as important once you move into the world of forced appreciation. You should absolutely never attempt such a project without first building a world-class team. You will need financing for your forced appreciation project, thus a mortgage professional. You'll need a real estate agent who understands the pre-repair and post-repair value, and you'll need a great team of renovators to keep your project within budget.

At times you can force appreciation simply by changing perception or use of a property. I already spoke about the highest and best use of capital. The same principle applies with real estate. Every property has a best use.

You wouldn't turn a downtown office tower into a boarding house. A higher and better use would be to put offices in an office tower. A more common (and achievable) example is a single-family home being converted into a duplex. Of course, this typically requires renovations, but the potential economic benefit of changing the use often outweighs the cost.

If the numbers work, forcing appreciation is often the simplest way to unlock capital after using the dormant equity in your own principal residence. Let's take a closer look.

Cosmetic Upgrades and the Mechanics of Forced Appreciation

Forcing appreciation simply means bringing a property up to its highest and best use. For example, you might find a rental property that's being rented for less than market rents. While doing your due diligence before purchasing, you might find out that the owner of your target property, a duplex, is charging $1,500 per month for per suite. By researching the rental market in the area and the property type, you might learn that the average rent is closer to $1,800 for similar suites. So you will have to do some more poking around. Why is your target building renting lower than market value?

This is a common situation. There are a couple of reasons for this. Sometimes my client and I will find that there is nothing wrong with the property. It's a simple case of the landlord not raising rents when he or she could have. We call these lazy landlords. Then my client will purchase the property and raise the rents as tenants turnover. Doesn't get much simpler than that.

But a more common scenario is one in which the same property will have un-mowed lawns, dated paint, worn out flooring, and maybe a few other small problems. Wear and tear happens, and properties get run down without consistent maintenance. The previous landlord may have let the property get worn and torn, and perhaps he or she didn't understand how this affects rental income.

The $600 per month in lost revenue is bad for the landlord's bottom line. That's $7,200 less in cash flow per year that the landlord could be making. But in failing to raise the rents, the landlord is losing out on far more than just a nice-sized bump in cash flow. Allowing income to be much lower than it could be actually affects the value of the property as a whole, because income and value are directly correlated.

You see, in real estate we have something called a cap rate (short for capitalization rate), which is an objective measure of the rate of return on a real estate investment property based on the expected income. We use it to estimate the investor's potential return. We calculate it by dividing the annual net operating income (NOI) by the current market value of the property. NOI is the income on the property minus all operating costs.

Capitalization rate = NOI ÷ current market value[25]

The interesting thing about the cap rate is that we can use it both as an objective measure, as the formula indicates above, and as a guideline for deciphering value. By dividing NOI by the current market value, you can calculate the objective cap rate, but by turning the formula around you can decipher the market value of a property. When we do this, we take a commonly accepted cap rate for a similar type of property in a similar area and calculate it as a percentage of the NOI to come up with the current market value. The calculation looks like this:

Current market value = NOI ÷ cap rate

So, by knowing the cap rates of a given property type in a given area, we can calculate how much property value the lazy landlord is leaving on the table. We know that he or she is leaving $7,200 per year on the table. That's $7,200 of NOI (because all expenses are already covered). Let's imagine this is a market in which properties are typically assessed using a 6 percent cap rate. Let's do the calculation:

$7,200 ÷ 0.06 = $120,000

The lazy landlord is leaving $120,000 of equity on the table simply by keeping rents low. Another way of thinking about it is in relation to carrying costs. If you can raise the income on a property by $700 per month, it means you can carry in the range of $100,000 worth of debt. (This assumes you had a 7 percent interest rate and were using a twenty-five year amortization which is more than twice the rate of borrowing at the time of this book being written.)

In many markets — especially strong markets — buyers will purchase properties that will pay for themselves. Thus, raising income by forced appreciation puts you in a better position to sell at a higher value.

Now, keep in mind a few things. First, these numbers are theoretical only. The actual value of a property is what the seller and buyer agree upon. In deals like this, which only require minor cosmetic upgrades, the seller is often well aware of the potential value improvement on the property. They won't always be willing to sell for the difference between what they are earning as a percentage of cap rate and the property's potential. But properties like this should always get you some kind of discount on purchase. If not, your real estate agent is failing you. Then all you have to do is raise rents and perform the minor cosmetic renovations, and soon you will have forced appreciation.

This "minor cosmetic renovations" situation is fantastic. Over the years, many of my clients (and myself) have taken advantage of this opportunity to create value. But another common situation is one in which the property requires some larger alterations to be put to highest and best use. As might be expected, there is often a bigger reward for this type of forced appreciation play.

Changing Use

Experienced investors often do larger forced appreciation deals, but if the deal is simple and clean enough, there is no reason why a less experienced investor can't also do such deals.

Not long ago I had a first-time investor client, Lin, who wanted to do a forced appreciation deal. When I meet a new investor looking to do a forced appreciation deal, I always pause to evaluate the person. I want to make sure they don't have any delusions about instant riches, so I ask them some questions and evaluate their motives.

You should expect this from a real estate agent. If you're looking for great team members but they don't ask you some questions back, you might want to find a new agent. It likely means they are transactional in their thinking. We'll discuss how to find a great real estate agent in more detail later.

After having a good conversation with Lin, I felt confident that her goals and motivations were aligned with my *modus operandi* and I decided to work with her. She wasn't a house-flipper and had no goal to become one. She knew about the power of forcing appreciation and wanted to capitalize by finding an under-used property and bringing it up to its highest and best use.

We eventually found a property for $350,000. Lin then put $60,000 worth of renovations into the property, which meant she had invested a total of $410,000. The purchase and renovation process took about two months to execute, and she found it very easy to put quality tenants into the property once it was renovated to a higher standard.

Sixty thousand seems like a big renovation, but for that amount of money Lin was able to add a second suite to the property. This dramatically raised the income on the property. A year later, Lin had the property re-appraised. She was pleasantly surprised to find that the property had appreciated by $80,000 — much of it forced. She had earned back her entire $60,000 renovation investment, plus a little extra. But, more importantly, Lin was able to re-finance the property and pull the money for a later investment, and her newly renovated property earned her more income since it had two legal suites.

Can you think of a better way to create that much value? This kind of scenario happens all the time in the real estate investment world. Of course, it only happens with detailed research, an excellent team, and access to capital. I don't want to give you the impression that this is easy or that it happens overnight, but I do want to share this example so that you can see the power of forced appreciation.

Renovations and this type of active real estate investing aren't a good fit for every investor or even most investors. Some investors, especially those later in their financial life cycle, would be dramatically better off purchasing a turnkey property — a property that's completely ready to rent, often with tenants already renting.

SELF-ASSESS YOUR REAL ESTATE PROFIT POTENTIAL

- Do you understand all of the ways to make money in real estate?
- Do you understand how mortgage pay-down helps you use the human tendency toward inertia to your advantage?
- Based on the examples in this chapter, which of the four real estate profit centres do you think are most profitable?
- Do you have the ability to not panic-sell in the event of a down-market year?
- Where do you stand on the risk continuum between turnkey property and change-of-use forced appreciation property?
- Based on your current goals, would you optimize your portfolio more for cash flow or market appreciation?
- Do you understand the relationship between market value and income?

PROFIT FROM REAL ESTATE

In this chapter, I wanted to give you a sense of how to profit from real estate. Of course, there are plenty of caveats. There are real risks and pitfalls, and, most important of all, every investor needs education and a great team. Caveats aside, there is nothing quite like real estate. It's incredibly consistent in its ability to create real wealth. I've been in the industry for decades now, and it never ceases to amaze me how consistent of a vehicle real estate is for wealth creation.

As I was writing this chapter, I reflected on examples of this consistency. My parents are the perfect example. My family moved to Canada back in 1968, and my parents bought their first house (in Toronto) for $11,000. They didn't earn a lot of money. Our family income at the time was only $2,000 per year. But fast-forward twenty-five years, and the family income had gone up to more than $100,000. While their income continued to rise, so did the value of their home. Today it's worth more than $600,000, a more than fifty-fold increase.

The value increase in their principal residence is just one piece of the wealth creation puzzle. If that property were a rental instead of their personal residence, they would have earned extra cash month after month for forty years straight. The compounding effect of that is remarkable.

Of course, there would have been ups and downs during those forty years of ownership, but, based on my own real estate investing career and the thousands of investment deals I've helped clients with, I can say with very few exceptions that this is a strategy that creates wealth.

It allows you to benefit from the enormous power of using leveraged money, and it is a stable, secure, and consistent method for growing wealth. Most importantly for retirees, it provides a monthly income that looks an awful lot like a pension during a time when pensions are, for the most part, nearly obsolete.

I can't recommend real estate enough as a profit vehicle — even with the caveats.

CHAPTER 9
Understanding Real Estate Expenses
by Simon Giannini

It's not what you make, it's what you keep.
— WEALTH CREATION MAXIM

WHAT WILL THIS COST?

Banks will only continue to lend money for further real estate purchases if an investor's debt service numbers are strong. Achieving this requires a solid degree of strategic real estate planning based on a strong understanding of the debt service formulas and real estate expenses.

Being highly leveraged brings greater returns. But none of the expected profit from real estate investments can ever be realized unless the property is sustainable over the long term. To be sustainable, a property must earn more than the sum total of its expenses. Additionally, the investor must plan for unexpected expenses. Thus, investors must assess risk and maintain reserve funds to see them through any rough patches that the market and property will produce over the course of ownership. Rough market swings are nearly guaranteed in the ownership cycle, but investors should not let these market swings scare them off. Prepared investors understand the inevitability of market swings and plan accordingly.

There are different types of real estate expenses. Some we must pay every month. Others we will only have to pay in an unlikely event. Regarding the second type: over a long enough time horizon, they eventually become likely events. This is why we plan our real estate expenses carefully and save money for the day the unlikely becomes likely.

In this chapter, we'll look at the various expenses — both constant and intermittent — that you will have to plan for as a real estate investor. As always, educate yourself further on expenses before choosing an investment. Make sure you have a complete picture of all the real estate expenses and income before diving in.

Preparing for the Unexpected with a Contingency Fund

In a worst-case scenario, you will want enough cash sitting in the bank to cover all the carrying costs of owning a real estate property for three to six months. Trust me, you want this much money, even if it's hard to imagine having to wait three months before putting renters back in the property. You might not have to wait for three to six months, but in the rare outlying case, you'll be hit with a large, sudden expense. Without the cash available in that moment, you will be in a very difficult situation.

A bad example of this was something I experienced one cold winter's night in Toronto, when the pipes burst in a multi-unit property I owned. Three of the units were flooded, making the property unlivable for the next several days. As a landlord, I had a contractual duty to house these tenants. They were not responsible for the pipes. I was. So I had to move them all into hotel rooms for the next couple of weeks while I fixed the burst pipe and cleaned up the property. I've never been more thrilled to have a large contingency fund than I was that night.

This is important to note because too many investors take the risk of not keeping such a fund. If you've gone for a couple of years without a catastrophe, you might be especially prone to this faulty thinking. People tend to think that just because something hasn't happened yet, it won't happen. Don't make the same error. Just as Calum has taught you to build a margin of safety into your borrowing-to-invest practice, you must also build a margin of safety into your real estate planning.

When you purchase a property, you will put three to six months' worth of money aside as a contingency fund. But you won't stop there.

Remember that you're only buying properties that create positive cash flow. You'll use some of that excess cash and continue to build up the contingency fund so that when major repairs like roofing (or, worse yet, an emergency) come about, you are prepared with the money.

Vacancy Planning

I like to treat vacancies as an expense that I plan for but don't usually pay. As of mid-2016, the vacancy rate is low in many strong markets in Canada. In Toronto it's 2 percent (according to the Canada Mortgage and Housing Corporation). When the numbers are tabulated and the overall number is a miniscule 2 percent, it means across an entire market. But if you own four units and have two vacancies at the same time, it means your effective vacancy rate at that moment is 50 percent. Also keep in mind that one month's worth of vacancy in a single unit rental, such as a vacant month between tenants, is equivalent to 8.3 percent for that property in that year (one divided by twelve).

Vacancies do happen from time to time. Most commonly, vacancies in a tight market, like the major Canadian rental markets, are just the result of turnover. One tenant leaves, and it might take you a month to do some minor maintenance and renovation on the property. During the turnover, you have a vacancy. Good landlords plan even for this eventuality and try not to have turnover times, but even the best are sometimes forced to.

When calculating yearly expenses, we usually double the vacancy rate. This means that in our yearly forecasts we treat that percentage of property income (double the market vacancy rate) as an expense. With a 2 percent vacancy rate in Toronto, I like to be conservative and use 5 percent in my calculations. So, if the property earns $50,000 in annual income, I will assume a vacancy expense of $2,500 (5 percent of $50,000). If you want to be hyper conservative, you can use a projection of 10 percent and assume a $5,000 expense. This way, when a tenant moves out and you have to paint and do minor repairs, then you've budgeted for the lost income expense. You will put aside extra money from cash flow to pay for minor renovations, like touch-ups between tenants.

Of course, some years you will have fewer turnover vacancies than others. In those years, the extra money will be like found money. But when the next year comes around and you're doing your planning, you had better prepare for a vacancy expense again. Always err on the side of caution.

Insurance

Remember the story about the flooded rental property? I was eventually reimbursed for the expense of putting up those tenants in hotel rooms.

The right insurance policy specific to a rental property will also cover you against the loss of rental income in the case of a bigger catastrophe, like if your property burns down. This is important, and a truly great and knowledgeable insurance broker will be a vital member of your real estate team. Failing to get the right type of policy might mean not being covered for things like loss of rental income.

Be clear with your insurance agent that you're insuring a tenanted property. One of the biggest problems I often see is an investor failing to mention there is a basement apartment in their property. They falsely think this will save them money on insurance rates, but they are putting themselves at huge risk. Lying to an insurance company is illegal and it could result in you not being covered at all. A lack of coverage would be just the beginning of your nightmare, since your lender may sue you for providing false information.

Insurance is a tiny price to pay to create peace of mind. It's the last line of defence between you and catastrophe.

Repairs, Maintenance, and Renovations

Renovations are a vital part of real estate investing. There are really two types of renovation. First is ongoing maintenance. Over the course of ownership and tenants moving in and out through the years, you will have normal wear and tear. The most common of these maintenance jobs are painting and flooring. They are a normal cost of doing business. The second type is capital upgrades. These are larger jobs that are done less often. You might only do a roof once every twenty-five or thirty-five years. You might upgrade a kitchen every decade or so.

For maintenance, it's important to plan your cash flow accordingly. Every month, grow your maintenance fund with money from cash flow so that when the inevitable maintenance issues come up, you have the cash on hand.

Capital improvements are often larger. You may plan to fund them with cash flow if the numbers work, but investors commonly use equity to fund larger capital improvements. After holding a property for several years, there is often built-up equity in the property. After consulting with your financial planner and mortgage professional, you may decide to use equity to fund another investment. This is great, but it often makes sense to also use some of that equity for large capital improvements.

These have enormous benefits. It's like servicing your investment portfolio. Imagine being able to directly improve your stocks. The management of them is entirely out of your hands, and you have to hope that the managers do a good job, but if you could, wouldn't you like to know that your investments are being modernized and upgraded where needed? The result of such expenditures is long-term viability and ultimately more profit, so long as the money is spent wisely. We have that ability with real estate. There is a direct correlation between profit and wise capital improvement spending.

For example, a couple of years ago I acquired a duplex with an unfinished basement. The plan was to renovate the basement and — as the upstairs tenants left — renovate the upper two units. But as soon as I renovated the basement, the tenants upstairs started having visions of beautiful new kitchens and bathrooms. They asked me if I would do it and I said yes, but renovating costs money, so I told them I'd have to raise the rent. They agreed. So I renovated the basement and then moved one of the upstairs tenants into the basement while renovating their unit. Once that was done, I moved the second tenant into the basement for thirty days while renovating their unit. I increased the rent on both upstairs units *and then* added a basement tenant. After all of the renovations, the cash flow and property value went up. After finishing the renovation I got an appraisal and found out that I'd gained $100,000 in active appreciation on the property. I spent $70,000 on the renovations, which meant a total net positive gain of $30,000 in value. It's important to note that the value went up so dramatically because of the increased income on the property as a result of adding the basement suite and raising rent on the other two suites.

I had budgeted for the capital expenditure in advance using equity from a different property and was prepared for the capital expenditure, plus I continued to charge rent during the renovation. I like this story because I think it demonstrates nicely how you have to plan capital expenditures and cash flow, but more importantly it shows how powerful well-timed capital expenditures can be.

What other investment do you know of would allow you to create that kind of money with a small amount of your own effort?

You have to plan for your capital expenditures when analyzing a property. Some properties create greater opportunities for improvement and, therefore, add value. A great real estate agent will be able to help you discover such properties, but your own education is key. Learn what those opportunities look like so you can recognize them when they're in front of you. Never go blind into a real estate deal. When you're inspecting your potential purchases, you must account for the potential capital expenditures and maintenance expenses. You'll need to know if the carpet is worn and may need to be replaced. Sometimes the tenant isn't planning on going anywhere and is okay with the worn carpet. You might have to replace it in six months or six years. You don't know when, but you know it will happen. Make sure you have the money on hand. Adjust your contingency fund accordingly.

Then there are the unexpected major expenses. On an older property, you may need an extra $10,000 suddenly. If the property is old, you would be wise to err on the side of a larger contingency fund instead of a smaller one.

New properties and different property types require smaller contingency funds. One of my new clients just bought a brand-new purpose-built multiplex. It's solid, new, and fully tenanted. He plans for a 5 percent vacancy rate, so he's covered there. Plus, the landscaping is smart hard-scaping. He doesn't need a large contingency fund as a percentage of income, but he's a smart investor. Over the years of ownership, he will re-examine his needs for maintenance and capital expenditures and plan his cash flow and capital wisely.

Property Management

You may want to self-manage your first couple of properties for a while to learn the business and save expenses, but over the long haul it won't make much sense for you to manage your own properties. I've already mentioned the simple systems you can put in place to ensure you place great tenants in your property. You will need to know the art of tenanting so that you can manage your property managers, but ultimately you want someone else doing that work.

Property management is one of the main reasons I see investors quitting the business. It can be difficult work, especially when managing multiple properties. One of the beautiful things about real estate is that you make money in your sleep. Most people find that it doesn't take too many property management calls before they start asking themselves if the money is worth it.

Even if you plan to manage your first couple of properties, it's vital to put a plan in place to hire a professional property manager as soon as possible. A good rule of thumb is to budget 10 percent of total income for property management, but it will depend on the property type and the area you live in. Ask your real estate agent about the correct numbers to budget for your property type and area. Also ask your real estate agent for property manager recommendations. A great agent will have trusted contacts in this area.

Accounting

You'll soon find that real estate investing makes your personal finance accounting more complicated, especially if your job was previously your only source of income. As a real estate investor, you'll have to separate expenses and capital improvements and consider the implications of earning more income. You'll have to keep capital gains distinct from regular income, and you'll be able to deduct a percentage of your interest expense on funds you borrow for investment purposes.

These and a thousand more accounting concerns explain why your accountant will become one of your most important team members. But accountants cost money. Actually, they're incredibly cheap compared to what you get from their service, but they do cost money, and it's important to treat their fees as a property expense.

The best place to find your real estate specialist accountant is in real estate investing circles. Your mortgage professional should have some great real-estate-specific accountants in his or her contacts.

Utilities

Wherever possible, you will want to pass along the utilities expense to your tenants. Making them responsible for their own consumption will ensure that they don't waste, but it will also give you certainty in your expense planning. It's difficult to plan for an expense that changes month to month.

Due to the way some properties are metered, though, you may not have the option of passing along all the expenses to your tenants. In such cases, you will have to add utilities to the rent. Don't let yourself be surprised by this. Failing to calculate utilities expense in advance and then failing to account for it in your rent could mean the difference between a cash-flow-positive property and a cash-flow-negative property.

Remember that cash flow is your lifeblood in real estate. The last thing you want is a property that requires you to pull money from your regular employment income to cover property expenses.

Financing

This is the biggest expense you will likely have. Obviously this is the topic of large swaths of this book, so I don't need to go into too much detail about it here. The thing to remember about financing is that it's like a volume knob. By turning up the volume (increasing financing), your property will have less cash flow. There are benefits to this. Lowering cash flow means lowering your taxable income. But if you're like Paul, whom you met in the last chapter, you'll want to turn up the volume and treat your cash flow income like your pension.

A common strategy for investors with long time horizons and no need for immediate cash flow is to use as much leverage as they can comfortably handle and amortize it over as long a time as possible. This minimizes the financing expense and helps improve cash flow.

The volume you prefer will have a massive impact on your expenses, but so will the interest rates. The main thing to keep in mind regarding interest rates is that, generally speaking, variable interest rate mortgages will save you money compared to fixed rate mortgages in the long run, but that at any given point in time you need to assess the risk-and-return trade-off of the two options.

Before choosing a variable rate mortgage, you have to decide whether you can psychologically handle the possibility of the interest rate going up. Lenders, for their part, prefer people to be in fixed mortgages to ensure certainty in cash-flow stability. Consult your mortgage professional to get a clear picture of the potential mortgage expense on your property type.

PROPERTY ANALYZER

Analyzing expenses is a vital part of real estate investing. Working the numbers is the core of successful investing, but you'd be surprised how simple it actually is, even if you've never had experience running a business. If you have rudimentary knowledge of Excel spreadsheets, you will have no problem analyzing and planning all of your expenses to ensure you have excellent cash flow. Even if you don't have such knowledge, don't worry. A great mortgage professional or real estate agent will be able to help you learn.

You can go to www.realestateretirementplan.ca to get your own working version of a property analyzer spreadsheet. Download it now and, for practice, plug in the numbers from a property you find on Kijiji or the Multiple Listing Service (MLS).

CHAPTER 10
Selecting a Real Estate Agent
by Simon Giannini

> If you think it's expensive to hire a professional to do the job, wait until you hire an amateur.
>
> — RED ADAIR

THE DIFFERENCE AN AGENT CAN MAKE

The right real estate agent can make or break your investing experience. Agents often hold massive influence over clients. This can (and should) be a good thing, because the right agent can potentially earn you many hundreds of thousands of dollars.

Of course, although the right team member can earn you a lot of money, the wrong team member can also cost you a lot of money. Selecting an agent who doesn't specialize in investments can result in you purchasing a property that doesn't perform well as an investment. Worse, you could end up with a massive expense on top of your poorly performing investment. Poor performers can sabotage the entire venture.

If you're reading this book, chances are that your goal is to improve and secure a better retirement. This will likely mean you have to purchase more than one property. But if the first property you purchase doesn't perform well as an investment, the entire venture might be thrown into question, since borrowing further money to invest becomes much more difficult if the debt service numbers are weak.

It's vital that each property works well, and the advice of a great real estate agent can make all the difference in finding, selecting, and executing the purchase of a great cash-flowing property. Unfortunately, some real estate agents have a transactional mindset. So long as they get the transaction (and, therefore, the commission), they don't think about what's best for the client. This runs counter to the purpose of real estate agents. Most real estate agents are great and don't have a transactional mindset, but there are some who do, and it's important to be aware of this.

Other agents don't have expertise in the investment realm. They will do their best, but without the requisite knowledge, they will find themselves in over their heads. There are dozens of factors to consider when selecting an investment property. Yes, you need to educate yourself and learn the answers to every one of your questions. But a great agent will also notice things that you might not.

A great team makes you look like a genius, which is why selecting your team members might be the most important decision you ever make — we're talking about hundreds of thousands or even millions of dollars toward your retirement. Of all the important decisions you need to make, this will be the wisest.

In this chapter I'll look at some of the important things to look for in an investment real estate agent. I'll start with a few key questions that will help you select a great agent. First of all, is he or she an investor? Second, does he or she understand the numbers of real estate investing? Third, does he or she have the connections and team to make your experience streamlined and successful? Fourth, is he or she an investment specialist agent? And fifth, does he or she have a solid reputation? By knowing the answers to all of these questions you will have the requisite information for selecting a world-class real estate agent.

EXPERIENCED, SPECIALIZED, REPUTABLE, AND INVESTED

Even if a real estate agent knows the theory of real estate investing well, I wouldn't trust him or her as my investment agent unless they were also experienced, specialized, reputable, and invested him or herself. There is nothing like real-life experience to create the compassion and understanding necessary for full service. An investor who has been in the trenches, gone through some market corrections, and seen how random occurrences like ice storms and flooded basements can affect real estate investments is the best kind of real estate agent.

When you've been in the business for decades, you end up seeing every kind of imaginable situation. Over the years, I've had many clients come to me for "clean-up" services, of a sort. By law I'm not allowed to tamper or interfere in any way with a deal that another real estate agent has under contract. But once the deal is done, the contract is over, and the client is experiencing the fallout from a poor decision or lack of insight, I'm then able to aid them.

One such client had purchased a property with another agent. The listing said the property was a legal duplex. After doing research and analysis, the client thought it looked like a pretty good deal, so he purchased it on the basis of what a legal duplex would earn. Seeing the price, he believed that he was getting the deal of the year, but in truth it was nothing more than a semi-detached two-storey property with an illegal basement suite in it. There is a significant difference between a legal duplex and a property with a basement suite, especially an illegal one.

This client had a friend who was a real estate agent, and when analyzing this deal his friend showed him renovated duplexes as comparison. But in our market, a duplex means two legal units above grade that conform to zoning.

Not only was this property not a legal duplex, but it also wasn't even a legal two-suite property. The client spent about $50,000 renovating the property with the expectation of adding about $150,000 of value to it. His plan was to then re-finance, pull out the cash he'd sunk into the property for renovations, and use the remaining cash to purchase another property.

When he tried to arrange financing, he soon found that the property was worth significantly less than he expected. He didn't even have enough equity to cover the entire cost of the renovation expenses. The value of an illegal two-suite property is far less than a legal duplex, so this shouldn't be surprising. It was surprising to the client, however, because the initial listing had claimed it was.

But it would be obvious to anyone with experience in investing that it wasn't a legal duplex. It was obvious to me when I first walked into the property, and it should have been to anyone who knew what they were doing — an agent who was also an investor, for example, would have warned the client immediately. The listing agent was either ill-informed or incompetent. The lawyers, not having visited the property, hadn't picked up on it either. The lawyer should have noticed, though, that the zoning said "single family." Perhaps he didn't realize the client thought he was getting a legal duplex.

There were mistakes, and when the dust settled the client had lost about $25,000 in cash alone, but that doesn't account for opportunity cost and time. The buyer's agent didn't know his stuff and, therefore, didn't protect the client. The seller's agent was wrong or unscrupulous or both. And in the end, when the tallies were made, it was the investor who paid the price.

This is why I always recommend a few things regarding experience: a) always choose a real estate agent who is also invested; b) always choose a real estate agent with several years of experience (at least five to ten years in the business); and c) always get a recommendation before choosing a real estate agent. If you follow these rules, you will avoid the majority of problems, like the one just described.

THEY MUST UNDERSTAND THE NUMBERS

As you've no doubt seen from the rest of this book, there are plenty of numbers to calculate in order to be certain you're getting a great real estate deal.

You should also be able to understand the numbers well. By using the spreadsheets provided at www.realestateretirementplan.ca, you'll be well on your way to accurately calculating the numbers. But it's also important to have a real estate agent who understands the numbers, too. An investment specialist agent who is also a neighbourhood specialist will give you deep insight into the projected numbers for ROI, cash flow, mortgage recapture, and appreciation rate in the neighbourhood.

A true specialist will know, for example, what the city is planning to do in the area. If a new subway or commuter station is being built within five years, a neighbourhood and investment specialist will understand the relationship of certain properties in proximity to the new subway stop.

If a large corporation is moving its offices to your region, a specialist will also be able to provide insight into the potential profit impacts to real estate. They will be able to provide helpful advice about which parts of town will be most likely to benefit from such developments.

This is the true value. You will massively benefit from an agent that has not just a grasp of the basic real estate investment numbers but also the deep knowledge of the type we just discussed.

But even the basic number crunching is valuable to you. Especially as you move up the ladder to start purchasing larger investment properties, it's vital to have an agent on your team who will give you a second set of eyes on your numbers. They will question you if they believe you've made false assumptions.

This can help immensely.

They will ask: What is the appreciation rate in the neighbourhood? What are the rents in the neighbourhood? What expenses will this property require in the coming months and years?

Make sure you select an agent with a deep understanding of all the numbers.

CONNECTIONS

The right agent, with deep experience and knowledge in your specific neighbourhood and investment type, will also be deeply connected. After many years in the industry, they've built up solid relationships with exemplary professionals.

For example, if you came to me first and were looking for an elite mortgage professional, I would send you to Calum. He would do the same in return. Because after decades in the business, and being committed to excellence the entire time, you soon realize that your own clients will succeed when you connect them to the best people.

We're in this business to help people, and nothing helps investors more than helping them build their power team. A great real estate agent will be someone who has connections to other great team members like mortgage professionals, lawyers, contractors, inspectors, accountants, and more. But connections go even deeper than just helping you look for other professionals. An agent with deep connections will also be able to help you uncover the deals you'd otherwise miss. A deeply connected agent will be able to find private sales, bank sales, sales from within their network, and, most of all, referrals from other investors.

One thing you'll soon realize once you start investing in real estate is that there are communities of investors in every major town across the country. There are multitudes of investment clubs, along with untold thousands of loose, unofficial networks of individuals meeting for coffee or beer. An agent will connect an investor to a mortgage professional, who will connect the same person to a contractor, who will connect to another investor, and soon everyone knows each other in one way or another.

There are great deals to be found via the normal means. Every agent can look on the MLS, but only a deeply connected agent will be able to bring you deals before they hit the MLS and those rare gems that could only be pulled off by them. This is why getting recommendations from other investors is one of the best ways imaginable to select a real estate agent. If you hang out in the right circles, you will start to hear similar things being said about certain agents. Once you surmise that a certain agent is putting together and finding a lot of great deals, you will know you're in the right place. Look for this intangible quality in a real estate agent.

QUESTIONS TO ASK WHEN SEARCHING FOR A REAL ESTATE AGENT

Many agents will claim to be experts, which is why you need to be knowledgeable enough to tell the difference between those who are truly expert investment specialist real estate agents and those who aren't. Use these questions as a guide to finding a great real estate agent:

- Are you an investor yourself?
- How long have you been investing for?
- How many properties do you personally own?
- How many properties have you helped investor clients purchase?
- How do you analyze an investment property?
- What types of investments are you most knowledgeable about?
- What are you looking for in an income property?
- How do you find properties (network, private, bank, MLS, other sites, referrals, etc.)?
- How do you meet with other real estate investors?
- Can you connect me with other team members in the area?
- How do you negotiate on a real estate purchase?
- Have you done any renovation deals?
- Have you done any turnkey deals?

THE POWER OF A GREAT AGENT

I recently did a deal for a client that illustrates what a highly experienced investment agent can do for you. I found a property with two retail storefronts side by side. Both had been vacant for some time, which meant that values were a bit depressed. Each one was listed for $300,000. The building was a single-storey retail storefront, but there were problems. For one, the façade was all wrong, and smaller rental spaces were a better fit for the area. The existing storefronts were each about 2,500 square feet, but since I specialized in the area, I knew that by turning them into smaller spaces, there would be more potential in the property. So, after consulting with my client, I decided to tie up the property with a sixty-day due diligence period.

Immediately, my team went to work creating a plan to turn the property into an executive office space with a bunch of different five-hundred-square-foot spaces that professionals could rent. I also knew that we would have to update the façade and then get leases in place. The goal was to do all of this *before* the end of the sixty-day due diligence period.

I'm proud to say we got it done. My team immediately made some renderings in order to market the building. Then we marketed the leases, negotiated them, and secured tenancies — all contingent upon the deal closing. We wanted to do it all in the sixty-day due diligence period because we wanted the client to have a high degree of certainty the property would be a great investment. Not much more security than a fully leased-up building before the sale is complete, is there?

Oh, and I forgot to mention — we also negotiated seller financing. We haven't spoken about seller financing yet in this book, but it's when a seller lends the buyer a portion of the purchase price, rather than the buyer getting it all from the bank.

After closing on the deal, my client and I went back to the bank for an appraisal and were happy to learn that the property was re-appraised at $800,000 based on the new leases put in place. The purchase price was $600,000 and the renovations cost a total of $150,000, which means that the client made $50,000 in forced appreciation.

But the best part was that the entire deal was risk-free. Remember that a sale isn't complete until the due diligence period is over and the conditions are released. We secured financing for the renovations, which meant the client didn't have to use his own cash, and the client even had the security of knowing the property would be fully tenanted *before* the deal closed.

A high-level real estate agent will have this kind of knowledge and the will to put together a deal like that. It's a unique set of skills. Just as the client in this example made lots of money because of my expertise ($50,000 immediately and much more over the long term), so will you benefit by choosing the right real estate agent. Don't take this process lightly.

CONCLUSION

by Calum Ross

I may not be there yet, but I'm closer than I was yesterday.

— José N. Harris

STEPS TO AVOID THE SIREN CALL OF INERTIA

Fans of Homer's *Odyssey* will remember the great scene in which Odysseus prepares for his journey through the land of the sirens by having his men tie him to his ship's mast to protect him from the irresistible call.

In today's world of personal finance, we are subject to a siren call no less appealing and still dangerous. We can tend to believe that since things have been a certain way for a long time, they will remain that way into the future. But reality continues to change. Sometimes it happens fast and we humans still fail to update our actions accordingly. One of the remarkable aspects of the Second World War was how slow the great powers were to recognize the danger coming out of Germany. As a result, they failed to take any meaningful action to stop the rising tide of Fascism, anti-Semitism, and aggression. The result was the Holocaust.

But that's an extreme example. More commonly, change is gradual, and only those closely studying the current trend alongside history will recognize the shifts as they take place. Being in such a position requires action. Even though most won't listen immediately, those with knowledge must act as an early warning system.

I consider myself in such a situation right now. Sure, retirement isn't as important or dramatic as a historical shift like war, but the change is real all the same. As we learned in Chapter 1, our ideas about and ways of securing a prosperous retirement are shifting. Due to large-scale pressures and changes, the traditional notion of retirement is no longer guaranteed for the majority of Canadians.

But as we learned in Chapter 2, at the same time there are tools and opportunities that haven't been historically available. The biggest difference is that it's up to the individual to take advantage of these opportunities, and the solution to Canadians' retirement woes is to borrow money and invest it as early as possible.

As we learned in Chapter 3, we must also beware of our false financial beliefs. Even with knowledge of the solution to our retirement woes, we are still at risk of subconscious self-sabotage. Take your financial education seriously, and also take the initiative to pass on sound financial knowledge to the next generation.

In this book I've outlined how borrowing to invest in real estate is one of the key solutions to upcoming retirement woes, but real estate must always be *part* of an overall financial plan, not the only solution. In Chapter 4, I laid out the major themes and issues involved in creating a sound financial plan and explained how real estate (and borrowing to invest) fit into that plan. Given the importance of having excellent financial planning advice, I also provided guidelines for selecting a financial planner.

My parents instilled in me the value of education. I firmly believe that power lies in the personal pursuit and acquisition of the right domain-specific knowledge. In Chapter 5, I sought to provide you with the same principles used by the wisest money managers on Earth. It's my hope you will seek to emulate their success with your own personal finances.

Armed with that knowledge, in Chapter 6 we moved onto a discussion of the advantages of borrowing to invest in real estate specifically. We learned how real estate as an asset class is perfectly suited to borrowing to invest and thus allows us to deploy more capital than any other asset class for normal retail investors like you and me.

Given the central importance of borrowing to invest, an investment specialist mortgage professional with financial planning training will always be one of the most important members of your wealth creation team. In Chapter 7, I outlined the requirement and method for selecting a world-class investment-specific mortgage professional.

With the personal education model outlined and the borrowing-to-invest groundwork laid out, Simon Giannini moved onto the real-estate-specific section of the book in Part 3. In Chapter 8, he laid out the simple but timelessly effective ways that investors profit from real estate. With this understanding, you can begin your deeper education and before long start taking action to profit from real estate.

But success in real estate, although not extremely difficult to comprehend, still requires careful financial projections and planning. Thus, in Chapter 9, Simon moved onto a discussion of the specific expenses involved in real estate. I'm confident it won't take you long to develop a working mastery over these concepts so that you can apply them in your everyday life, but first you need to be aware of the basics of real estate expense planning.

Just as a financial planner and mortgage professional are vital members of your team, so is a world-class real estate agent. In Chapter 10, Simon discussed the criteria to use when selecting an investment specialist real estate agent. Of course, there should be other members of your team, but once you have the "Big Three" in place, the others should come more easily.

I hope this book is a beginning of your personal finance education and of you taking action, not an end. Given that, a legitimate question is what to do next.

PERMISSION TO FAIL AND NEXT STEPS

Of all the things I want you to take away from this book, perhaps the most important is the permission to fail. People who know me often have the false belief that I have it all figured out, and the truth is that I really don't.

Just like you, I still lose money on my stock portfolio from time to time, and even with the best resources I still sometimes buy into real estate markets shortly before they fall in value. While I have gotten better at this as time goes on, it still pains me to lose money. But I have gotten better at not reacting impulsively when I do.

Just like the world's biggest investment banks, we all have the same wealth constraints. We all have a limited amount of financial capital (money on hand), and we all have a limited amount of incoming capital (income). To optimize wealth we must, just like the investment banks, focus on increasing our after-tax income and invest in assets that yield the greatest after-tax rate of return.

Part of the personal financial journey for all of us is the inevitable small failures along the way. When you're in the arena, you will take a few blows. I've never seen a Stanley Cup championship team make it there without a few cuts and bruises. But a well-thought-out, consistent strategy with the right team in place while taking plenty of action will get you a heck of a lot closer to your goal than remaining stuck in inertia.

I want to emphasize the well-thought-out part.

Please also don't confuse this book as permission to cash in your RRSP to buy real estate today. I fundamentally believe in diversification and looking closely at asset allocation. My personal RRSPs are maxed out, and I invest every penny of those funds into stocks, bonds, and money market investments.

The right professional advice is the most powerful next step you can take. While it is unsexy to say, personal financial success begins and ends with a good budget and an excellent financial planner. Despite the fact that I am a financial planner myself with two finance degrees, I still do not manage my own money. When it comes to someone who can fact-check my financial planning and keep me on track with my financial well-being, I put my money where my mouth is. My financial planner manages my RRSPs, TFSA, and RESPs.

Beyond diversification, having a solid portfolio of non–real estate investments is a key part of being able to borrow money. As you build a real estate portfolio, lenders like to see that you have liquid non–real estate investments. In fact, many mortgage lending credit-risk departments want you to have no less than $50,000 in investable assets outside of real estate for every property you own. They do this for two reasons: 1) they want to see investment diversification so you don't get into financial trouble; and 2) they want you to have the backup liquidity to endure a surprise maintenance cost or short-term tenant strife. If you call our office or follow our system, we will make sure you are not put at risk.

Once your financial plan is taken care of by a great financial planner, and you have a clear mortgage plan with the aid of a mortgage professional, then you can turn your attention to real estate. Your first step will be to find an investment specialist real estate agent. I run all my deals by Simon Giannini. Truth be told, I actually idolized Simon to some extent before we started working together. When I entered the mortgage industry, I saw Simon's name and presentations all the time, and I remember thinking, "Wow, that guy is about as good as they get." Interestingly, now, after working with Simon for a number of years and looking after many clients together, my perspective has definitely changed. Whereas I used to *think* he was as good as they get, today I *know* he is as good as they get.

I trust him to be my second set of eyes on all my deals, and I regularly use him as a resource for market data and the most up-to-date real estate stats. Whether you are buying or selling your principal residence or building your real investment portfolio, you will be hard-placed to find a realtor who has more expertise, negotiation skills, and commitment to customer service than Simon and his team. You need Simon, too, or your own version of Simon, if you want to have real estate investing success.

I felt the need to close by emphasizing the importance of your personal team. By far the single biggest determining factor in succeeding with your financial goals is working with a great team with a common vision.

I read over twenty personal finance and real estate books a year and I hold a B.Comm. and MBA in finance, as well as two financial planning credentials, yet there has not been a single time I've consulted Simon or my other team members when I haven't learned something new or benefitted from a unique way of looking at an issue.

I know in the years ahead I will likely endure more financially challenging times and have my fair share of life issues the same way everyone else does. What I don't do now is worry about my financial well-being. If all my investment assets and real estate holdings do is perform at the average rate, then I know that between Simon and the others I will always have a great team that has my best interests at heart.

I wish you all the best success for a happy, healthy, and high-quality life that is relieved of the unnecessary burden of worrying about money. If you follow the system in this book and engage the contacts I have mentioned, I have every confidence that you will be more than just fine.

ACKNOWLEDGEMENTS

To all my clients: over a decade ago I became fiercely committed to becoming one of the greatest personal finance minds of our time, but it's the thousands of people I have served who have really given me the practice to develop and grow my knowledge. Without your fabulous support, I would not have arrived where I am today.

Francis Tapon (PhD, Duke University, and MBA, Columbia University) taught my first finance class and made it interesting. I can't speak highly enough of all the great professors and students I studied with at Harvard Business School and the Schulich School of Business. I can't say how much I valued the opportunity of studying with you. You all do smart at a whole different level and have made me realize what human beings are capable of.

I'd like to acknowledge my friend and mentor Todd Duncan, a *New York Times* bestselling author and the world's top mortgage trainer. I'm the only Canadian he has ever directly mentored, and having him train me has given my global mortgage banking and customer service knowledge an almost unfair competitive advantage. You are an amazing human being.

I have to thank Don R. Campbell for the wealth of literature, training, and insight on real estate investing he has given me. The knowledge and wisdom you have on this topic is truly impressive.

I would like to thank Kathryn Lane, Dominic Farrell, Kirk Howard, and Carrie Gleason at Dundurn, as well as Jenny Govier and Zander Robertson. Without your efforts, this book would never have come into the world.

I'd also like to thank my ex-wife, Michelle Card. We chose not to remain together as a married couple, but I am forever grateful for your dedication to and love for our daughters. You are a great mother and it is very much appreciated. Thank you.

I'd like to thank my mom and dad, who both left Scotland to bring my sister and me to Canada for a better life. Like good Scottish parents, you taught me the value of a dollar by always making me work for my allowance, never letting me compromise on my GPA, and, above all else, repeatedly demonstrating the value of determination. Failure wasn't an option in my house when growing up. I owe much of my success to the integrity and work ethic you demanded from me at every part of my upbringing.

I also have to thank my two daughters, Abigail and Alexis. Being a divorced dad has made being a great father even more important to me. Words cannot properly express the deep love I have for you both. You inspire me to be a better person.

GLOSSARY

Appreciation	an increase in monetary value.
Availability bias	the tendency to only use the limited knowledge presently available for decision-making.
Bonds	a type of debt security in which the issuer pays interest (the coupon) to the purchaser.
Cap rate (capitalization rate)	the ratio of annual net operating income (NOI) to the asset value of a real estate property.
Cash flow	the money that the owner of a real estate property retains after all property expenses are paid.
CFP (Certified Financial Planner)	a respected Canadian professional financial planning designation.
Compound interest	interest calculated on the initial principal and also on the accumulated interest of previous periods.
Coupon	interest payments received by bond owners.
Debt conversion	the practice of shifting personal mortgage debt into investment debt as the principal of a mortgage goes down.

Debt service	the cash required to cover the repayment of interest and principal on a debt.
Depreciation	a decrease in monetary value.
Dormant equity	accumulated home equity that's not being used to invest.
ETF (exchange-traded fund)	a type of security that tracks an index, commodity, bonds, or basket of assets. It doesn't have excessive fees attached to it, as mutual funds often do.
Forced appreciation	using renovations to push up the value of a real estate property.
GIC (guaranteed investment certificate)	a type of low-risk, low-reward investment that offers a guaranteed rate of return over a fixed period of time.
GDS (gross debt service)	the percentage of a borrower's income needed to cover housing costs. Banks typically want the borrower to remain below 32 percent on this measure.
HELOC (home equity line of credit)	a lending product offered by banks in which home equity is used as the security.
IIROC (Investment Industry Regulatory Organization of Canada)	the national self-regulatory organization that oversees financial trading.
LTV (loan-to-value)	the ratio of a real estate purchase's financing to its value. Typically banks permit a maximum of 80 percent financing on real estate investment properties.
MBA	a master's degree in business administration.
MLS (Multiple Listing Service)	a co-operative real estate service for brokers to share listings and commissions.

Mortgage pay-down	the process of paying down mortgage principal with each monthly payment. Equity builds this way.
Mutual fund	a professionally managed investment fund shared by several smaller investors.
NOI (net operating income)	the sum of all of a real estate property's income, minus its operating expenses.
PFP (Personal Financial Planner)	a respected Canadian financial planning designation.
Re-advanceable mortgage	a sophisticated loan product that issues new debt as principal is paid down. These loans are often broken into different segments, which make them useful for a borrowing-to-invest program.
REIT (real estate investment trust)	a company that owns income-producing real estate. These companies can be publicly or privately owned.
Reserve fund	money set aside by real estate investors, and added to, for every property purchased. The money is to be used for expected or unexpected future expenses.
RESP (Registered Education Savings Plan)	a tax-free savings plan designed specifically to be used to pay education expenses at a later date.
ROI (return on investment)	the benefit to an investor of some previous investment made. A sum of money, in the case of a financial investment.
RRSP (Registered Retirement Savings Plan)	a tax-deferred savings plan designed specifically to be used to support retirement.
Smith Manoeuvre	a debt-conversion financial strategy made famous by author Fraser Smith.

Stress test
the calculation of what future expenses (especially interest) might be if certain conditions change for a real estate investment. Stress testing is considered a prudent practice for all investors before they purchase an investment.

TDS (total debt service)
the percentage of a borrower's income needed to cover both housing costs and other monthly financial obligations. Banks typically want the borrower to remain below 40 percent on this measure.

TFSA (Tax-Free Savings Account)
a government-registered investment account in which all gains are tax free, even when withdrawn.

TSX (Toronto Stock Exchange)
Canada's largest stock exchange.

Turnkey property
a property that is ready to be used as an investment without any alterations or changes from the day it's purchased.

TVM (time value of money)
the financial principle that states that money available at the present time is worth more than the same amount of money at a later time.

NOTES

1. Libby Kane, "These 3 Charts Show the Amazing Power of Compound Interest," *Business Insider*, July 8, 2014, www.businessinsider.com/amazing-power-of-compound-interest-2014-7.
2. "Canadian Household Saving Rate, 1981–2016," *Trading Economics*, www.tradingeconomics.com/canada/personal-savings.
3. "Canada Pension Plan," *Wikipedia*, https://en.wikipedia.org/wiki/Canada_Pension_Plan.
4. "Canada's Big Banks Earn $35B in Profits for 2015," *CBC News*, December 3, 2015, www.cbc.ca/news/business/bank-profits-rise-1.3348661.
5. Paul Brent, "Don't Let High Management Fees Drain Your Portfolio," *Globe and Mail*, November 22, 2013, www.theglobeandmail.com/globe-investor/funds-and-etfs/etfs/high-management-costs-drain-away-portfolio-growth/article15561239.
6. Matt Egan, "86% of investment managers stunk in 2014," *CNN Money*, March 12, 2015, http://money.cnn.com/2015/03/12/investing/investing-active-versus-passive-funds.
7. "Investment Funds in Canada (IFC)," Canadian Securities Institute, www.csi.ca/student/en_ca/courses/csi/ifc_info.xhtml.
8. Blair W. Keefe and Peter A. Aziz, "Canada Introduces New Mortgage Prepayment Disclosure Rules," Torys, March 9, 2012, www.torys.com/insights/publications/2012/03/canada-introduces-new-mortgage-prepayment-disclosure-rules.
9. Rob Gerlsbeck, "Pensions: A Broken Promise," *MoneySense*, Dec/Jan 2010, www.moneysense.ca/save/retirement/pensions-a-broken-promise.
10. "How Does a Defined Benefit Pension Plan Differ from a Defined Contribution Plan?" *Investopedia*, April 7, 2016, www.investopedia.com/ask/answers/032415/how-does-defined-benefit-pension-plan-differ-defined-contribution-plan.asp.

11. "Comparing Retirement Options," Healthcare of Ontario Pension Plan (HOOP), http://hoopp.com/Learning-Resources/Defined-Benefit-Plan/Comparing-Retirement-Options.

12. "Warren Buffet," *Wikipedia*, https://en.wikipedia.org/wiki/Warren_Buffett.

13. Ben Bernanke, "Why Are Interest Rates So Low?" Brookings Institution, March 30, 2015, www.brookings.edu/blogs/ben-bernanke/posts/2015/03/30-why-interest-rates-so-low.

14. "Dow Jones — 10 Year Daily Chart," *macrotrends*, www.macrotrends.net/1358/dow-jones-industrial-average-last-10-years.

15. "Efficient Frontier," *Investopedia*, www.investopedia.com/terms/e/efficient-frontier.asp.

16. Claire Boyte-White, "What Are Some Examples of Different Types of Capital?" *Investopedia*, March 27, 2015, www.investopedia.com/ask/answers/032715/what-are-some-examples-different-types-capital.asp.

17. "Time Value of Money — TVM," *Investopedia*, www.investopedia.com/terms/t/timevalueofmoney.asp.

18. Rob Carrick, "Real Estate or Stocks — Which Will Make You Richer?" *Globe and Mail*, April 4, 2014, www.theglobeandmail.com/real-estate/mortgages-and-rates/renters-make-for-wealthier-investors/article17834799.

19. Talbot Stevens, "Clarifying Tax Deductibility When Borrowing to Invest," http://talbotstevens.com/Resources/Leverage/StratSheets/2001MYClarifyingTaxDeductibilityWhenBorrowingtoInvest.htm.

20. "Speculation," *Investopedia*, www.investopedia.com/terms/s/speculation.asp.

21. "Investing," *Investopedia*, www.investopedia.com/terms/i/investing.asp.

22. Rob Gerlsbeck, "Pensions: A Broken Promise," *MoneySense*, Dec/Jan 2010, www.moneysense.ca/save/retirement/pensions-a-broken-promise.

23. Rob Carrick, "Real Estate or Stocks — Which Will Make You Richer?" *Globe and Mail*, April 4, 2014, www.theglobeandmail.com/real-estate/mortgages-and-rates/renters-make-for-wealthier-investors/article17834799.

24. One of the best Canadian resources for learning how to analyze regional and neighbourhood appreciation potential is still Don R. Campbell's *Real Estate Investing in Canada: Creating Wealth with the ACRE System* (Mississauga, ON: Wiley, 2009).

25. "Capitalization Rate," *Investopedia*, www.investopedia.com/terms/c/capitalizationrate.asp.

RECOMMENDED READING

To download the tools and resources mentioned in this book,
go to www.realestateretirementplan.ca.

Aitken, Sandy. *Mortgage Freedom: Retire House Rich and Cash Rich.* London, ON: Insomniac, 2011.

Ayers, Ian, and Barry Nalebuff. *Lifecycle Investing.* New York: Basic Books, 2010.

Bach, David. *The Automatic Millionaire, Canadian Edition: A Powerful One-Step Plan to Live and Finish Rich.* Toronto: Doubleday Canada, 2009.

———. *The Automatic Millionaire Homeowner, Canadian Edition: A Powerful Plan to Finish Rich in Real Estate.* Toronto: Doubleday Canada, 2008.

Beyer, Thomas. *80 Lessons Learned: On the Road from $80,000 to $80,000,000.* N.p.: Prestigious Properties, 2013.

Campbell, Don R. *81 Financial and Tax Tips for the Canadian Real Estate Investor: Expert Money-Saving Advice on Accounting and Tax Planning.* Mississauga, ON: Wiley, 2010.

———. *Real Estate Investing in Canada: Creating Wealth with the ACRE System.* Mississauga, ON: Wiley, 2009.

Campbell, Don R., Kieran Trass, Greg Head, and Christine Ruptash. *Secrets of the Canadian Real Estate Cycle: An Investor's Guide.* Mississauga, ON: Wiley, 2011.

Campbell, Don R., and Patrick Francey. *The Little Book of Real Estate Investing in Canada.* Mississauga, ON: Wiley, 2013.

Campbell, Don R., and Peter Kinch. *97 Tips for Canadian Real Estate Investors 2.0.* Mississauga, ON: Wiley, 2011.

Chilton, David. *The Wealthy Barber: The Common Sense Guide to Successful Financial Planning.* Toronto: Stoddart, 2002.

————. *The Wealthy Barber Returns.* Kitchener, ON: Financial Awareness Corp., 2011.

Foster, Sandra E. *You Can't Take It with You: Common-Sense Estate Planning for Canadians.* Mississauga, ON: Wiley, 2006.

Gardner, Stephen E. *Doctor Your Retirement: How the Smartest Doctors Build Wealth with Real Estate.* Mississauga, ON: Wiley, 2006.

Graham, Benjamin. *The Intelligent Investor: The Definitive Book on Value Investing.* New York: Harper Business, 2006.

Gray, Douglas. *Making Money in Real Estate: The Essential Canadian Guide to Investing in Residential Property.* Mississauga, ON: Wiley, 2012.

Gray, Douglas, and Peter Mitham. *Real Estate Investing for Canadians for Dummies.* Mississauga, ON: Wiley, 2010.

Hagstrom, Robert G. *The Warren Buffett Way.* Mississauga, ON: Wiley, 2013.

Kiyosaki, Robert. *Rich Dad's Guide to Investing: What the Rich Invest in that the Poor and the Middle Class Do Not!* Scottsdale, AZ: Plata Publishing, 2012.

Lechter, Michael A. *OPM: Other People's Money: How to Attract Other People's Money for Your Investments — the Ultimate Leverage.* New York: Business Plus, 2005.

Smith, Fraser. *The Smith Manoeuvre: Is Your Mortgage Tax Deductible?* N.p.: Outspan, 2006.

INDEX

Page numbers in italics indicate an illustration.

8 percent income, 140

accountants, 116, 127, 147, 184
accreditation, need for, 97
after-tax costs, 89, 93–94, 143, 170
after-tax rate of return, 117–20,
    143, 170
analysis paralysis, 80–81
    and capital, 152
appreciation, 71, 114, 120, 133,
    135, 139, 141, *142*, 161, 169–
    71, 182
    See also forced appreciation
asset classes, 75
    real estate as, 74, 76–77, 86,
        98–99
availability bias, 79

balance sheets, 96, 136
banks
    investment advisors, 32–34
    as lenders, 153

profit levels, 30–31
Bernake, Ben, 54
Big Five banks, 30–31, 33
bonds, 19, *26*, 130
borrowing, after tax costs, 89
Brent, Paul, 32–33
broken paradigms, 66–67
Buffett, Warren, 50, 129
buy signals, 121

Canada
    deficits and surpluses, *57*
    Income Tax Act, 116–17
    rates of return in, 143
    tax laws, 116
cap rates, 173–74
capital, 152, 159
    cost of, 94
    debt, 104–09, 134, 153
    defined, 103–04
    equity, 107, 134
    questions about, 123

capital gains, 165, 168
  See also taxes
cash, 105, 109, 114
cash flow, 91, 118–19, 130–31,
  139, 167, 185
  positive, 163–65
  projecting, 145–46, 165–66
cash flow planning, 151–52
cash flow properties, 114–15
central banks, 54
cognitive dissonance, 11–12
compounding interest, 20–21, *22*,
  65, 82
consumer debt, 56
Consumer Price Index, *55*
contingency funds. *See* reserve
  funds
costs of borrowing, 105
CPP (Canada Pension Plan), 18,
  27–29, 39
CRM (Client Relationship Model)
  legislation, 31–32

debt
  bad, 56, 110
  corporations using, 95–96
  good, 57
  government, 56
  paying off, 137
  servicing, 129–30, 133, 144,
    153, 178
  as a tool, 62, 95, 168–69
debt capital, 104–09, 111, 134, 169
"debt is evil," 11, 62, 81–82
debt-to-equity ratios, 35
deficits and surpluses, in Canada, *57*

defined benefit pension plans,
  18–19, 37–38
defined contribution pension
  plans, 18–19, 37–38
diversification, 88–89, 115, 122,
  160
dormant equity, 12, 47, 49, 64–65,
  93, 105, 114, 118, 131, 147, 159,
  169
doubling penny thought experi-
  ment, 20–21
downsizing, 24–25
downturns, 127

equity capital, 108, 134
equity market returns, 26
ETFs (exchange-traded funds), 33
expenses, 145, 164–66, 178–85
experience, in a financial planner,
  97

false beliefs, 60, 104, 196
fear of knowledge, 74–75
financial capital, 106–09
financial education
  lack of, 17, 62, 113
  need for, 61
financial literacy, 35
financial mental models, 84
financial planners, 34, 49, 115,
  163–64, 196
  balanced portfolios, 94–95
  commission-based, 85–86, 98
  fee-based, 98, 127
  selecting, 96–99
financial plans, 86–87

fixed-rate mortgages, 36
flight, tendency towards, 121
flipping, 172
forced appreciation, 161, 171–76,
182, 193–94
forced savings, 137, 162
fund managers, 33

government debt, 56
greed, 30, 123–24
guidelines
advice, 127
long-term strategies, 128–29,
170
margins of safety, 127–28
for selecting properties, 133

HELOCs (home equity line of
credit), 45–46
hold cycles, 142
home values, 71
household income, 93

IIROC (Investment Industry
Regulatory Organization of
Canada), 33
image-based decision-making,
82–83
impulsive decision-making,
67–69, 123
income, questions about, 10
Income Tax Act, 116–17
industrial model of government,
62
inertia, 195–96
inflation, 53, 54, 55, 91

insurance, 146, 181
interest, 116, 118
interest rates, 54, 57–58, 143
high, 52, 53
low, 42–43, 53, 134
investing
borrowing and, 11–12, 42–43,
45, 49–51, 63–64, 86,
125–26
stock market, 19, 70, 74, 88–90,
92, 114 15, 129, 135
vs. speculation, 121–22
investing early, benefits of, 22
investment advisors, at banks,
32–33
investment horizons, 128–29
investment loans, 128
investment portfolios, returns on,
23
investment real estate, and mortgage professionals, 149–53

lazy money, 113–14, 137–38
lending, 108, 127
leverage, 18, 44, 114, 117, 125, 128,
153
leveraged loans, 134
liabilities, 129–30
things as, 12, 117
lines of credit, 49
See also HELOC (home equity
line of credit)
liquidity, 93, 128–29, 144
loans, 53–54, 129–30, 134
long-term returns, 114
long-term strategies, 128–29

management fees, at banks, 31–32

margins of safety, 127–28, 179

market appreciation, 169–71

market corrections, 75–77, 120–21

market cycles, 142

market lulls, 142

market returns, 51

Markowitz Efficient Frontier, 89

mass affluence, 133, 136

mathematical thinking, 20–21

mental modelling patterns, 61, 70, 84

middle-class mindset, 73–74, 137

Mike's analysis, 140

minimum-wage work, after retirement, 18, 83

money paradigms, 60

monthly coupons, 91, 93, 135, 138–39

mortgage providers/professionals, 153

  choosing, 149–53

  interviewing, 154–55

mortgages, 34, 36–37, 104, 131, 185

  analyzing, 162–63

  for investments, 63–64, 114, 135

  paying down, 160–64

  re-advanceable, 42, 48

  refinancing, 35–36, 66, 132, 136, 169, 176

  traditional, 41–42

  in the U.S., 115–16

Muffet and Bunger example, 107–09

Mutual Fund Dealers Association, 33

mutual funds, 33–35, 87–88, 92, 136

negative cash flow, 137

NOI (net operating income), 174

non-real estate assets, 114

Ontario, tax rates, 105

passive real estate investments, 94

pension funds, 10, 37–38, 86

pensions, 11, 18–19, 136, 139, 148, 160–61

portfolio approach, 93–95

portfolios

  balanced, 86, 94, 115, 196–97

  and real estate, 89, 92–93

  See also bonds; diversification; equity market returns

precautions, 127–29

principal protection, 90

principal residences, 48, 71, 115, 117, 132, 137, 169, 177

profits

  and banks, 30–31

  from real estate, 135, 160–61, 177

property managers, 73, 78, 144–45, 147, 164, 183–84

property selection, 133

quality-of-living downgrades, 25, 83, 152

questions

  on capital, 123

dormant equity, 147
for mortgage professionals, 154–55
for real estate agents, 192
real estate profit potential, 176
retirement opportunities, 58
retirement risks, 39
QWERTY keyboard example, 66–67

rates of return, 25–26, 90, 106, 135
ratios
debt-to-equity, 35
income-to-purchase, 140
real estate
benefits of, 88–91
as get-rich-quick scheme, 122, 151
real estate agents, 77–78, 146–47, 166, 172, 175, 184, 187–94
real estate assets, 66
real estate collapse warnings, 71, 75–77
real estate growth, 71
region selection, 171
REITs (Real Estate Investment Trusts), 92, 94, 152
renovations, 175–76, 181–83, 193
rental income, 129–30, 132, 173
rental rates, 140
reserve funds, 144–45, 179–80
retail investors, 67–70, 121
retirement
defined, 9
goals of, 93
retirement opportunities, 58

retirement planning, 19, 39, 151–52, 160, 169
retirement risks, 39
retirement system, 25, 40
returns, low, 25, 26, 27
risks
awareness of, 96, 141–42, 153, 185
mitigating, 93, 121–22, 141, 168
and returns, 128–29
ROI (return on investment), 47, 106–09, 162
Rosentrenter, Kurt, 32
Royal Bank, 95–96
RRSPs (Registered Retirement Savings Plans), 18, 50, 198

S&P 500 returns, 27
savings rates, 23
security, 129–30
self-assessments
financial mental models, 84
real estate profit potential, 176
retirement opportunities, 58
retirement risks, 39
self-education, 79–80, 121–22, 156, 171
sell signals, 121
seller financing, 193
services related to financial planning, 99
short-term financial decisions, 21–22
speculation vs. investing, 121–22, 161

strategies, debt-conversion, 48

tax accountants, 116
tax deductions, 43, 49, 64, 82, 89,
    93–94, 106, 115–18, 132
taxes, 89, 119–20, 128, 136, 170,
    172
teamwork, 77–78, 99, 119–20,
    146–47, 149–53, 160, 166, 172,
    175, 183–84, 187–94, 196–97
tenants, 72–73, 80, 130, 144–45,
    161, 179, 181–82, 185–86
TFSAs (Tax Free Savings
    Accounts), 18
time horizons, 92–93, 96, 170
time value of money, 17, 19–23,
    105, 109–10, 112

timeless principles, 122
Toronto, 139–40, *142*, 170, 180

United States, 115–16
U.S. Federal Reserve, 54

vacancy rates, 180
volatility, 88

wealth creation, 43, 104–05
    and capital, 152
    through real estate, 71
wealth creation principles, 17
worst-case scenarios, 65–66, 129,
    143–45

ABOUT THE AUTHORS

CALUM ROSS

Calum Ross has funded over $2 billion in mortgages since 2000, helping to create more than $1.8 billion of incremental net worth for his clients. He has personally funded more than 6,000 mortgage transactions. As a keynote speaker across Canada and the U.S., he has also appeared as an expert in various media, including BNN, the *National Post*, and the *Globe and Mail*. He is an alumnus of Harvard Business School and holds an MBA in finance from the Schulich School of Business. He lives in Toronto.

To learn more about Calum and his team's services, visit www.mortgage management.ca, or contact Calum's office directly by emailing clientcare@mortgagemanagement.ca or calling 416-410-9905. Or, you can join more than 10,000 others and follow Calum on Twitter — @CalumRossTO — where he shares daily insights on real estate, mortgages, and all things personal finance. If Facebook is more your style, you can follow his page, Calum Ross Mortgage (facebook.com/calumrossmortgage).

SIMON GIANNINI

Simon Giannini is a thirty-year veteran of the real estate industry and one of the highest-producing brokers in Canada. Host of *The Real Estate Talk Show* on CFRB 1010 AM and the TV show *Real Estate Intelligence*, he is a sought-after commentator and has been featured on BNN and in the *Toronto Star* and the *National Post*. Simon lives in Toronto.

To learn more about Simon Giannini, visit www.therealestatecentre.com. You can also email him directly at simong@reccanada.com or call his office at 416-366-9090.

To download the tools and resources mentioned in this book,
go to www.realestateretirementplan.ca.

dundurn.com dundurnpress

@dundurnpress dundurnpress

dundurnpress info@dundurn.com

DUNDURN